# DEMONIAC

NATHAN KRUPA

# DEMONIAC

© 2020 by The Almoner.
All rights reserved.

First Printing, 2020.

ISBN-13: 978-1-7327487-6-7 (PAPERBACK EDITION)
ISBN-13: 978-1-7327487-4-3 (KINDLE E-BOOK EDITION)
ISBN-13: 978-1-7327487-5-0 (EPUB E-BOOK EDITION)

10 9 8 7 6 5 4 3 2 1

The Almoner
P. O. Box 6805
Augusta, GA 30916–6805
thealmoner.com

Ordering Information:
Orders by U.S. trade bookstores and wholesalers.
Please contact Ingram Content at www.ingramcontent.com

Available in E-Book.

The Almoner™ and the associated logo are Trademarks of The Almoner.

Book Design by Catholic Way Publishing.

# DEDICATION

*To my mother, whose tireless love, sincere faith,*
*countless prayers, and boundless generosity made all*
*the difference.*

# THANKSGIVING

*I give thanks to God for my salvation and for the journey that inspired this book. I thank my wife and family for their faithful support and encouragement. Thanks go to Mary Vizzini my editor and interlocutor for asking the right questions, to Peter Vizzini for his graphic design talents, and to Christina Alexander for her inerrant red pen. The stories chronicled in this book would never have happened without the generosity of my parents, sisters, and my Alleluia family. Thanks also to Golden Harvest Food Bank for giving me the opportunity to live the Gospel in my professional life. Special thanks go to Mike Firmin, my Virgil on my journey out of the great abyss.*

# CONTENTS

# FOREWORD

"DEMONIAC" IS A LITTLE BOOK about one man's journey. It is large, however, because it is about a wayfarer — an identity all of us share. Like some big books in the western canon of literature, the oral tradition preceded any scripted work. Nathan told the story of "Demoniac" to me some years before I read it. In the pages that follow, although some of the natural charm and pathos of the orator might be missed, you will still encounter his transparency, passion for living well, and genuine love of others. It is his love for you that produces the fruit of this published work.

"Demoniac" is particularly challenging for the modern reader because it professes with unwavering conviction that demons exist and attack us. It is tempting to write off Nathan's account as a type of monomania. After all, didn't he suffer a psychotic break? Insanity as a medical illness has substantial street credit while the acceptance of demonic influence is rare. Yet for Nathan the difference between demonic activity and mental illness is not controversial, academic, or culturally sensitive. It is fact. You may find yourself taking a side.

Nathan's dark wilderness of mental and spiritual affliction is a tale of intense suffering. Most of us have never personally experienced insanity nor plumbed its depths of terror, anguish, shame, and disorientation. Nevertheless, a sensitive reader of "Demoniac" may vicariously experience the horror present in Nathan's account of his descent into madness.

As a psychiatrist in my tenth year of practice, I am professionally astounded by his recovery. Indeed, the psychiatrist from the inpatient unit where he was admitted after a psychotic episode fully expected that he would require medication for the rest of his life. His prognosis, based on the severity of the episode, was sound. The truth, however, confounds the prediction. I testify that Nathan is quite sane, without the assistance of medication, and has been living happily for many years.

Despite the unsolvable puzzle that his story presents to my professional mind, I cannot ignore the outcome and I will not deny the quest. A record of his journey into that frightening mental state is collecting dust in a medical records room in California. Meanwhile, the protagonist of that record is unrecognizable; he is a dramatically different man. Here is some good news for us all: the person we are today does not have to be the person we are tomorrow.

For the serious and sensitive reader, this little book is more than a sensational memoir or oddity of intellectual interest. It is a witness to hope and the power to change. Wherever you find yourself on the spectrum of belief, I hope you will lower your defenses long enough to meet the man and hear his testimony. He may challenge us, but he has hope to offer; the darkness is not so great that a light cannot penetrate it.

> "The light shines in the darkness, and the darkness has not overcome it."

If you cannot believe his explanation for the phenomenon he describes, meet it with your own explanation. At the same time, try simply to rejoice with him and share in his joy. Our fellow man was lost and is found; he was blind but he now sees! He has passed through an inferno, he has found his Beatrice, and his heart sings for love. Before you venture forth into "Demoniac," savor the sweet words of the poet Dante, the first twelve lines of his comedy. Let the timeless introduction to the poet's own transformative journey serve as a pithy segue into Nathan's:

> *"Midway along the journey of our life*
> *I awoke to find myself in a dark wood,*
> *for I had wand ered off from the straight path.*
>
> *How hard it is to tell what it was like,*
> *this wood of wilderness, savage and stubborn*
> *(the thought of it brings back all my old fears),*
>
> *a bitter place! Death could scarce be bitterer.*
> *But if I would show the good that came of it*
> *I must talk about things other than the good.*
>
> *How I entered there I cannot truly say,*
> *I had become so sleepy at the moment*
> *when I first strayed, leaving the path of truth …"*

Dante's Inferno — Canto I

PATRICK MOLITOR, MD

# CHAPTER I

# Demoniac

*At once, a man from the tombs who had an unclean spirit met him. The man had been dwelling among the tombs, and no one could restrain him any longer, even with a chain. In fact, he had frequently been bound with shackles and chains, but the chains had been pulled apart by him and the shackles smashed, and no one was strong enough to subdue him. Night and day among the tombs and on the hillsides he was always crying out and bruising himself with stones.*

(MARK 5:2-5)

NOBODY EVER READS THIS part of the Gospel and says, "That guy! I want to be like *that* guy!"

Yet there I was. Stark naked on a stranger's front lawn in the middle the night. Pounding my head into the ground to wake up Mother Earth, just like the voices told me. Thankfully, a quieter voice told me to do it on the grass instead of in the middle of the street so I wouldn't hurt my forehead.

After I finished sucking the evil magic off my fiancé's diamond engagement ring, I planted it in the ground, believing that an enormous bush covered with beautiful engagement rings would sprout from the spot. The quiet voice suggested that I put my clothes back on before I returned to my apartment.

Does this sound crazy? My fiancé thought so, too. When I woke her up to tell her that I had planted her ring as a seed of our love and she could find it if she followed the yellow brick road, she was not amused. She broke up with me via a restraining order.

I ended up in the hospital, and the doctors put me on sedatives that knocked me out for three days. They hoped to undo some of the damage that nine days without sleep had done to my mind, but despaired of my recovery. They thought my mind would never recover from a psychotic break so severe. Minds that broken don't, and they were experts.

They were also wrong. Medical science couldn't cure me because I had a problem that it doesn't admit exists. I was not simply a madman. I was a demoniac.

You see, my fiancé dabbled in witchcraft and the occult. Tarot cards, crystals, books on witchcraft and new age spirituality littered our apartment, which, since I was an atheist, made no difference to me so long as we continued our mutual interests in sex and marijuana. I didn't realize that my soul was slowly filling with legions of demons.

I know. I never would have believed it either. When I experienced a demon leaving my body with a wave of projectile vomiting and a sensation like being electrocuted, I was astonished.

Most scientists — let's face it, most people — say that belief in demons is a relic of the dark ages. They don't say this because they have proof that demons don't exist. They say this because they just can't find them. Demons are not something that you can measure with a ruler or thermometer. They don't follow predictable rules like those in chemistry and physics, where $FeO_2$ = rust and $E=mC_2$. Demons are immaterial creatures, with a tendency to be uncooperative, if not downright . . . diabolical. When confronted with the question of demons, honest scientists will usually throw up their hands and say, "Umm, we really don't know, but quite frankly the idea freaks us out, so we'd rather not talk about it."

Don't get me wrong. Science is great for understanding the physical universe, but it is illogical to claim that nothing exists except that which can be examined by current scientific tools. It's kind of like saying that bacteria didn't exist before scientists created the microscope. "We can't find them" is not the same as saying, "They don't exist."

In my case, my problems weren't simply biological, so I didn't just need a doctor. I needed a Savior. A Deliverer.

> Catching sight of Jesus from a distance, he ran up and prostrated himself before him, crying out in a loud voice, "What have you to do with me, Jesus, Son of the Most High God? I adjure you by God, do not torment me!" (He had been saying to him, "Unclean spirit, come out of the man!") He asked him, "What is your name?" He replied, "Legion is my name. There are many of us." (MARK 5:6-9)

I grew up Catholic, but I always put the stories from the Bible and the lives of the saints on roughly the same level as the science fiction and fantasy that I loved. Catholicism struck me as little more than a set of rules that I (kind of) believed and that kept me from doing a lot of the fun things that I saw my friends doing. Never did I imagine that it was *all* true and that God could speak. Then He spoke . . . to me.

I can almost hear you thinking, "This crazy guy wants me to believe that one of the voices in his head is God?" It's hard to describe the difference between the voices I heard driving me to destruction in the depths of madness and the voice of God. Imagine the demonic as a loud, raunchy heavy metal concert chanting a litany of self-destruction. The voice of God is more like the sound of your dad whispering to you as you awaken from a horrible nightmare. It's a voice that you recognize in the very depth of your being, even though you can't remember ever hearing it before.

The diabolical choirs brought untold misery and destruction into my life. The voice of God brought peace, healing, and deliverance. He gave me hope, which had vanished in the whirlwind of insanity.

> . . . the unclean spirits came out and entered the swine. The herd of about two thousand rushed down a steep bank into the sea, where they were drowned . . . (MARK 5:13)

I wish my recovery had been this easy, but Jesus did not choose to cast out all the demons at once. Maybe there weren't any pigs nearby. Or maybe He knew I wouldn't have learned an essential lesson. It's one thing to cast a demon out. It's an entirely different thing to *keep* it out.

Instead of casting the legion into the swine, God threw me into the coliseum to do battle with one demon at a time. But He empowered me with His Holy Spirit and armed me with the name of Jesus. He gave me a love of prayer and Eucharistic adoration. He brought wise counselors to aid me in the fight. He raised me from the dead in the sacrament of confession, and gave me the infinite blessing of communion with Him in the Most Blessed Sacrament.

After God spoke to me in the middle of the night, I started a twelve-year war with the devil, during which I would cast out one demon only to have him return with back up, and the fight would get harder.

My whole life had to change. If I wanted to be free of the evil one, I had to learn to live a life of virtue. I became a professional beggar, raising money to feed the hungry. I married a woman who had spent three years in a convent. I joined a Christian community. I reconquered my soul from the devil's control one demon, one vice, at a time. This battle will continue until the day I finally face my Savior, my Judge, my Redeemer.

> ... As he was getting into the boat, the man who had been possessed pleaded to remain with him. But he would not permit him but told him instead, "Go home to your family and announce to them all that the Lord in his pity has done for you." Then the man went off and began to proclaim in the Decapolis what Jesus had done for him; and all were amazed. (MARK 5:18-20)

I'm alive today because of Jesus Christ. I am sane because His power is real. My healing was not simply *a* miracle. It was a succession of extraordinary miracles too numerous to count. I will share some of those stories with you, and I think you will be amazed. You might be skeptical. I'm pretty sure you'll be entertained. I hope that what I have learned during my combat with the evil one will help you fight your spiritual battles. Learning to recognize the attacks of the evil one against you and how to respond using divine weapons might change your life.

# CHAPTER 2

# The Fall

*Now the snake was the most cunning of all the wild animals that the Lord God had made. He asked the woman, "Did God really say, 'You shall not eat from any of the trees in the garden'?" The woman answered the snake: "We may eat of the fruit of the trees in the garden; it is only about the fruit of the tree in the middle of the garden that God said, 'You shall not eat it or even touch it, or else you will die.'" But the snake said to the woman: "You certainly will not die! God knows well that when you eat of it your eyes will be opened and you will be like gods, who know good and evil."*

(GENESIS 3:1-5)

HOW DID I END UP naked on that stranger's lawn?

My first steps toward madness were like the Fall of Adam and Eve in slow motion. Rather than one BIG mistake that got me cast out of the garden, I took a slow, voluntary journey into darkness. I was like a disobedient child following a trail of candy out of the playground into the hands of a lurking predator.

The devil knew my weaknesses from the beginning because they have been Man's weaknesses since the Beginning. Plant a seed of doubt, stir up a desire for forbidden fruit, and set the snares. His evil work done, he watched and waited. I did the rest. It's almost embarrassing how easy I made it. His traps were so sweet, so seemingly innocuous, right until the moment that he snatched me up and carried me away.

Satan first planted the seed of doubt, "Does God exist at all?" The answer seems so obvious to me now. Of course, how could He NOT exist? But I didn't have that rock-solid certainty growing up. I wanted God to exist, but more at the level of a sky fairy who makes everything awesome all the time — the false vision of God that some atheists mock so fiercely.

I also had a love for science and had a hard time sorting out whether I should believe what I heard from my priest or my science teachers. Was I supposed to believe that Adam and Eve were the first human beings, or that people were the result of evolutionary processes that played out over tens of millions of years? It never occurred to me that they could both be true, or that divine revelation and scientific investigation could exist harmoniously.

The devil's first attack on man is to contradict God's revelation. You might notice this within the story of the Fall itself. "You certainly will not die," says the serpent, as if to say, "Look at the beauty of the fruit before your eyes. Believe the sweetness that fills your nose." The first sin took place in their minds: believing the serpent instead of God.

Starting with the Enlightenment, the devil's lie was to suggest, "What you call divine revelation is nothing more than mythology . . . fairy tales."

I heard that lie echoed in thousand forms. The devil is in the marketing business, so I heard it from teachers, celebrities, in books I read, during the movies I watched, shouting from every direction, "All religion is a fantasy, an opiate to dull the pain of fools." And as if by magic, all my faith in divine revelation vanished in a puff of smoke.

> The woman saw that the tree was good for food and pleasing to the eyes, and the tree was desirable for gaining wisdom. So she took some of its fruit and ate it; and she also gave some to her husband, who was with her, and he ate it… The Lord God then called to the man and asked him: Where are you? [Adam] answered, "I heard you in the garden; but I was afraid, because I was naked, so I hid." Then God asked: Who told you that you were naked? Have you eaten from the tree of which I had forbidden you to eat?"
> (GENESIS 3:6,9-11)

Pornography was my forbidden fruit — at once pleasing to the eyes and desirable for the pleasure that it would give me. I was in second grade when I saw my first Playboy, and that first glimpse festered into an addiction that would last 20 years. I started back before the Internet, so I needed to find physical copies of pornographic magazines and movies if I wanted to satisfy my addiction. It was surprisingly easy. Once the Internet got rolling, I had a whole world of pornography at my fingertips.

Jesus said, "Blessed are the pure of heart, for they shall see God." The opposite is also true: "Woe to the impure of heart because God shall become invisible." It's a spiritual principle that the devil understands completely. Impurity, especially sexual impurity, darkens our minds so that it becomes more and more difficult to see the hand of God until we're completely blind to God's existence.

The consequences of my actions were eerily similar to the story in Genesis. When Adam and Eve ate from the forbidden fruit, they were filled with shame and hid from God. I experienced that same sense of shame and desire to hide. Pornography and the sins that come with it are secretive. Shameful. I didn't want anyone to know about it because I knew it was wrong.

Of course, I justified my behavior to myself by saying that everyone does it, which is largely true. That truth didn't make me feel any better, but it gave me a reason to ignore the guilt and shame.

> The Lord God therefore banished him from the garden of Eden, to till the ground from which he had been taken. He expelled the man, stationing the cherubim and the fiery revolving sword east of the garden of Eden, to guard the way to the tree of life. (GENESIS 3:23-24)

The sad thing is that God didn't have to kick me out of the garden. I walked out on my own. In high school, I'd done a lot of acting in school plays, so I decided to study theater at a Jesuit University in Los Angeles. A highway to Hollywood. The Catholic pedigree of the school gave my parents some comfort, but in the end it was armor made of tissue. I indulged in all manner of heathenry.

The moment I left my parents' house for college, I stopped practicing my faith. I thought that I was exercising my freedom. I exulted in my ability to sleep off my Saturday-night hangovers instead of getting up for Church on Sunday. I had no idea what I was leaving behind. Sin piled onto sin.

At the time, I thought freedom from religion was great. I

went to a lot of parties. Found work on a bunch of different theater productions as an actor, technical director, director . . . you name it. I sang in Carnegie Hall with the University choir.

Now, I look back on my college years and early twenties with a mixture of sorrow and regret. Only two moments stand out in my mind.

On two separate occasions, two different girlfriends asked me the question, "What would you do if I were pregnant?" Each time I told them, "We will get married and raise our child together." They never spoke of it again.

Only looking back years later can I see that they might have been, probably were, saying, "I am pregnant. What should I do?"

When I think about two children who might have been, my heart aches. There might have been others. I grieve for them and their mothers and for putting women in a position where they felt they had to make a "choice."

The Fall bears fruit in death. God warned me. I refused to listen.

# CHAPTER 3

# Repossessed

> *"When an unclean spirit goes out of someone, it roams through arid regions*
> *searching for rest but, finding none, it says, 'I shall return to my home*
> *from which I came.' But upon returning, it finds it swept clean and put in*
> *order. Then it goes and brings back seven other spirits more wicked than*
> *itself who move in and dwell there, and the last condition of that person is*
> *worse than the first."*
>
> (LUKE 11:24-26)

BAPTISM STARTS WITH AN exorcism. God makes room for the Holy Spirit to move in. Mortal sin, however, serves the Holy Spirit an eviction notice. God won't dwell in a person who willingly chooses grave sin. As I chose to commit mortal sin after mortal sin, I got further and further from God. My house was swept and empty. What could possibly go wrong?

Almost immediately after graduating from college, I realized two very important and disturbing facts:

1. A bachelor's degree in theater is practically useless when

it comes to finding meaningful employment. It might actually count against you.

2. Student loan companies don't care.

I had to find a job. I used a temp agency and quickly found a job as an assistant at Creative Artists Agency, one of the biggest talent agencies in Los Angeles — no, the world.

Fame and fortune that I'd only seen on TV or in movies swirled around me daily. The biggest movie stars, directors, and writers would show up at any time. Money poured through the place like the Mississippi River.

I was thirsty.

They paid me $10 an hour to be an agent's assistant, just barely enough to keep body and soul together if I stole stale bagels for lunch from the conference room. They justified the pay by saying that they had a line of 100 people waiting to take my job, which was true. Many people would step over their dying mother to work at CAA and start building the relationships they needed to become Hollywood moguls.

To say that this environment is not conducive to the spiritual life is perhaps an understatement, but I wasn't interested in being spiritual. I was interested in being fabulously rich and famous (or at least close to rich and famous people).

I never went to any of the fabulous Hollywood parties where I could hobnob with the rich and famous. The thing that you never hear about Hollywood is that 98% of the people in Hollywood are poor nobodies desperately trying to be rich somebodies. They spend their time like I did, answering someone else's phone, scheduling someone else's lunches, and picking up someone else's coffee. The vast multitude of Hollywood lackeys has their own, more modest versions of the Hollywood parties, in hopes of being ready when they finally graduate to the big leagues.

But what was happening to me spiritually during this time? Well, the devil and his seven nasty friends came back to visit and decided to stay. One of the secrets of the spiritual life that Hollywood movies miss is that the devil prefers the subtle to the dramatic. He'd rather use a stiletto than a bazooka.

At first, the demonic infestation came in the form of temptations that led me deeper and deeper into sin. Greed, lust, sloth, pride, anger, vanity, and envy. Seven spirits more wicked than the first. All found their place in my heart.

Temptation is the devil's primary weapon against every person. Each time I succumbed to temptation and fell further into a particular sin, the devil got one more hook into me. The more I sinned, the more hooks landed, and the more enslaved I became to sins. The sins became habits of vice that no longer required the prompting of outside temptations. Sin became a part of me, but I was oblivious. I was pretty much an atheist at this point, so the word sin didn't mean anything to me. I thought I could define good and evil to suit my own tastes.

I didn't stay at CAA much more than the obligatory year before moving to another entertainment company. It was all a part of "paying my dues," as all the books on Hollywood say. You only climb a ladder by spending some time on the bottom rungs. Then my life took a dramatic detour.

When I was 25, my old college roommate showed me a prototype digital 3D display he built from junk lying around his apartment. He flipped a little switch, a disk started spinning, and BOOM, suddenly three multicolored balls jumped out into the air. You could look around and see the sides of each one. It was the coolest thing I had ever seen.

We decided that we should leave Hollywood behind and become tech billionaires. We formed a company, and I used that little homemade contraption to convince a law firm to take a small piece of that company in exchange for $300,000 in legal services. On paper, I was suddenly a millionaire.

Unfortunately, paper millions don't pay the bills. I had to work several side jobs to make ends meet, and after three years of work, when we uncovered patents that were filed six months before ours, the tech company completely unravelled. My partners and I decided to close the company and go back to regular life. So depressing.

During those years, I met a gal. We hit it off and decided to move in together. I grew to love her very much and eventually proposed marriage. She accepted. There was only one problem...

She was into new age spirituality and the occult. We never talked much about it, because I had become an aggressive atheist. I rejected everything that couldn't be explained by the physical sciences as idiotic superstition. We agreed to disagree, and I didn't mind that she kept things like tarot cards, crystals, and books on new age and witchcraft around the apartment. I thought it harmless at best and foolish at worst.

I couldn't have been more wrong. Practicing exorcists agree that dabbling in the occult opens the door for the devil to begin operating in extraordinary ways. Testimonies report everything from psychological disturbances — bizarre sensations, disembodied voices, extreme emotions, and disordered behaviour — to supernatural manifestations — levitation, wounds appearing from nowhere, and demonic voices speaking in unknown

languages through a person's mouth. Just picking up and shuf-
fling a tarot deck is enough to crack open that door. The demons
that already had infested me invited all their buddies to come
throw a party and burn their house down — by which I mean
me. Eventually, they made their move.

I remember the first steps into madness very clearly. My
fiancé and I watched a movie called *The Secret,* based on a book
that has sold something like 30 million copies. The main idea
of the movie is that your thoughts become reality. If you think
a lot about having a big house, then the universe will manifest
a big house for you. If you think a lot about your dream career,
the universe will manifest your dream career. The movie bor-
rows ideas and terminology from quantum physics to paint the
universe as a kind of magic genie that will bring you whatever
your heart desires.

It's quite a stupid idea, as the billions who are living in
poverty might tell you. But they package it in such an attrac-
tive way that it makes you want to believe. Let me repeat: the
book has sold 30 MILLION copies. Some weird things also
started happening that seemed to reinforce the idea, things
that I took to be evidence that what the movie described was
true. In retrospect, I can only remember one of these incidents.
I expressed my desire that people would start calling me "boss,"
and very shortly after, the attendant at the gas station did so.
Looking back, it sounds so stupid, but at that moment, I was
like "WHOAH! It's all true!"

The false logic of the movie broke my mind. I wanted to put
my hope in something after the failure of my business. I remember feeling so much joy and happiness about *The Secret* that I
couldn't sleep . . . for nine days. I was filled with unexplainable

energy and couldn't stop thinking about the strangest things. My mind spun completely out of control.

Describing insanity from the inside is difficult, even when looking sanely back at it. It gets all jumbled up and out of order. For years I couldn't even think about that time without starting to feel sick and just a little crazy. Something snapped inside my mind, and I was suddenly unable to distinguish between fact and fiction. Fantasy novels were as real as biographies; dragons and magicians were as real as bankers and engineers. I have a hard time remembering events and their chronological order, but I'll try to give you a picture of how crazy I was. I already mentioned running around naked and burying a diamond ring. It got worse.

I spent an afternoon walking barefoot around Beverly-wood (a neighborhood in Los Angeles), allowing the wind to determine my direction. The old Irish proverb "Let the wind be always at your back" popped into my mind, and it seemed like a good idea. I changed direction whenever I felt the wind shift. I have no idea how long I was walking or how far I traveled, but by the end of it, I had holes in the soles of my feet that took three months to heal.

I decided that I wanted to have perfect vision, so I broke my glasses in half as a sign of my commitment. Of course, my vision didn't improve the least little bit, but boy was I excited.

I danced on a manhole cover in a cul-de-sac for an hour, singing "Let the Sunshine in" from the musical *Hair* at the top of my lungs. A neighborhood security guard stopped me after about half an hour but seemed convinced that I was sane when I told him that I was only dancing. He left and returned a little later to tell me that it was time for me to go.

Around this time, my fiancé told me that I wasn't making

sense, to which I responded, "No, I'm making *non*-sense!" like that was a perfectly acceptable alternative.

I spent an afternoon flooding our bathroom, wearing a blue pouch with stars on it as if it were a sorcerer's hat. I took all of my fiancé's various lotions and painted the bathroom Jackson Pollock style. To this day, I can't go into a Bath and Body Works because of the memories the smells trigger. This incident happened near the end of the madness, but I vaguely remember that I thought it was part of me bringing all of the dead back to life.

Near the end of the nine days, I concluded that I was the star of the old movie "The Truman Show." You'll recall that it's about a man whose entire life is a television show and all the other people merely actors. I decided that it would be good for ratings if I stopped trying to control my temper and got as angry as I could with my fiancé, without crossing the line into violence. I'm sure I was terrifying.

The last night that I ever saw my fiancé, I went out for a walk and found the cops waiting for me when I returned. They handcuffed me and tried to put me in the back of their squad car. I asked them why. They said because they wanted me in the back of the car. I responded that I hadn't done anything. They told me they wanted me in the back of the car. I asked why. They finally agreed to let me stand behind the car in cuffs as I watched the woman I loved walk out of my life forever.

After the LAPD released me, I walked around a while, picking up bits of garbage and eating them. I took my favorite guitar out of my apartment and smashed it against a telephone pole because it radiated evil. I "realized" the sun had died and would never come up again. My friends found me in my apartment wearing nothing but a towel repeating, "Help me, I'm lost. Help me, I'm lost." I don't know how long I'd been there.

I spent three days in a hospital on heavy sedatives. I remember waking up and telling my sister and the nurse, "All I want is to love her." My love for my fiancé was the only true thing that I knew. Nothing else made sense to me. It kept the wolves at bay and my mind from completely disintegrating. The mental hospital was like a horror movie. Those white walls are a blank canvas for all kinds of terrors.

I didn't have health insurance, so the hospital released me after a few days. The madness itself lingered for weeks; my mind didn't function correctly anymore.

My sister and her husband kindly took me into their home. Several days after being released, I told them that I was Puff the Magic Dragon. Later that same night, I snuck out of their apartment and walked several miles through the darkened streets of Los Angeles to my parked car. I got in and drove 800 miles to a little town in the Arizona desert. No one had any idea where I had gone. No one could contact me because I had ripped my phone in half. Because it was evil.

I thought I would find my fiancé in the desert because that was where she grew up. She would be hard to locate, though, because she might be wearing someone else's body. I borrowed some random stranger's phone and left her a message, so my family learned my location.

I went to a bar to look for her, and in the bathroom saw a poster showing hands in different attitudes of prayer. For some reason, the picture inspired me. I started imitating those gestures, forming them over and over again. Hands in prayer, mind in confusion, soul in darkness.

I spent the night at a hotel, and the next day I ran into my ex-fiancé's little brother. He gave me a place to stay for the night, and I returned to Los Angeles the next morning.

On the way back to my sister's house, I stopped on the bluff where I went to college and had a conversation with the devil. It's possible that this happened completely in my imagination. I was totally crazy. I sat down on a bench overlooking the city next to what I thought was the devil. He started talking to me like he was expecting me. He looked like an older white man with a thick eastern European accent. I felt heat radiating from him, and when I looked at him, my mind filled with an image kind of like the Eye of Sauron.

"Look at that mess," he said, gesturing at the city. "What a pile of garbage. They should burn it to the ground and start over."

I tried to defend Los Angeles, saying that they just needed someone who had some vision, who could get people to work together. They could transform the city into something beautiful.

He laughed at that. He told me that his wife was in the church going to Mass, but he couldn't stand the place. So he waited outside. After a little more chit chat, the bells on the tower rang. We walked together to greet his wife. I don't remember seeing another person anywhere on the campus.

My good friends helped me move all my stuff out of the apartment that I had trashed during the breakdown. They didn't know that I insisted on doing it at night because I didn't want the sun to know where I had moved. My grasp on reality was slippery.

Then I received the restraining order. I would go to jail if I ever tried to contact my (former) fiancé again. That killed my hope of ever seeing her again. The weight of sorrow felt like a corpse sitting on my chest.

A few weeks later, I climbed to the top of my sister's 13-story apartment building with my heart set on a final flight attempt. My entire being vibrated. It's hard to describe the feeling of chaos devouring you from the inside. Insanity. Despair. Confusion. Anger. Bitterness.

Looking out over the city, mental images of leaping over the railing and splashing on the ground below filled my mind. I tried to hold the barking thoughts at bay and admire the beauty of the city lights from above, but thoughts of self-destruction crashed against my mind. I wanted nothing more than to put an end to the misery that was devouring me.

Then my sister's iPod started playing KT Tunstall's song "Another Place to Fall." The lyrics say, "See yourself as a fallen angel . . . find another place to fall." About halfway through the song, I heard a tremendous WHOOMP that sounded like a car crash above me. I remember thinking at the time that it was the sound of an angel being knocked out of the sky. The building is the tallest for blocks around, so I have no idea what caused the sound.

The pressure to kill myself vanished. Perhaps at that moment, God looked at me and had mercy. If I had died that night, I would have been lost to Him forever. I know I didn't deserve mercy. Maybe someone out there was praying for me. Probably my mom.

I walked calmly down the stairs. That night, I had the first restful sleep I'd had since the beginning of the madness. That climb down the stairs was the beginning of a very long road to recovery.

CHAPTER 4

# Conversion

*As he was leaving Jericho with his disciples and a sizable crowd, Bartimaeus, a blind man, the son of Timaeus, sat by the roadside begging. On hearing that it was Jesus of Nazareth, he began to cry out and say, "Jesus, son of David, have pity on me."... Jesus said to him in reply, "What do you want me to do for you?" The blind man replied to him, "Master, I want to see." Jesus told him, "Go your way; your faith has saved you." Immediately he received his sight and followed him on the way.*

(MARK 10:46-52)

INSANITY CAN BE COMPARED to blindness of the mind. Truth becomes hidden. The mind gropes around in darkness, grabbing onto various things, not knowing what it's touching. I remember thinking that I should be able to turn the lights on just because I started thinking about it. I would become very confused when what I wanted didn't happen.

While talking to a psychiatrist, the understanding dawned on me that my ability to tell the difference between what was real and what was fantasy had broken. She responded, "Yes, that's what we call a psychotic break."

While living with my older sister, I saw the psychiatrist for a month or two . . . until the money ran out. She put me on a powerful anti-psychotic named Zyprexa. The dose was enough to knock down a horse. I slept a lot, which probably helped.

My plight reminded me of the Russell Crowe movie, "Beautiful Mind." In that movie, a brilliant mathematician suffers a very similar psychotic break. He decides to use his beautiful mind to filter out the true from the false. Except that it doesn't work, at least not completely. I ignored that part and decided that I would give it a shot.

I tried to sort through my crazy experiences, putting some into the true box and the others into the crazy box. I tried to put a big lock on the crazy box. Unfortunately, this process had very little effect on my emotional state. I was terribly volatile. Anger, depression, confusion, despair — a storm of negative emotions swirled through me.

My mother came out from Georgia to California to visit me. She listened patiently to all my craziness for a couple of days. Something weird caught my attention, though. When she put her arm around me as we were strolling around the apartment complex, her hand burned unpleasantly hot on my side. I didn't understand that till later. Her visit ended and she returned to Georgia.

The psychiatrist told my family that I would have to be institutionalized. People who go through psychotic episodes as severe as mine never recover. I had no health insurance, though, so I was set adrift when my bank account was empty. My grandmother and uncle paid out of pocket for counseling and drugs for a couple of months, but it cost a fortune, so they had to stop. I had to stop taking meds and going to the psychiatrist, and I never went back to the hospital.

My sister and her husband owned and operated a black box theater in LA, where they taught and performed improv comedy. I idled a lot of time away sitting in her office. One day I noticed a Bible sitting on a shelf. For some reason or another, I picked it up and sat down to read.

I read the whole book of Proverbs in one sitting. It's not too long and filled with common-sense, practical wisdom. "The man of violent temper pays the penalty; even if you rescue him, you will have to do it again" (PROVERBS 19:19). Who could disagree with that? I had just experienced the truth of it.

I remember feeling a little better after reading it, although I can't tell you why. Perhaps truth is the only real antidote to insanity.

Unfortunately, my sister's charity reached its limit after a couple of months, and she asked me to start looking for a job so I could move out. This prospect terrified me. I don't think she understood the chaos, anger, and despair that still raged inside me. I put together my resumé and managed to land a few interviews. I'm pretty sure it took less than two minutes for the interviewers to realize that I was unstable — really unstable.

I couldn't stay, so I moved in with my old roommate's family in Oregon. They are good people. My roommate (the mad scientist inventor from the failed business venture) and his brother were starting a coffee roasting business. They had built another contraption that used a bunch of mirrors to concentrate the heat from sunlight to roast coffee beans.

The problem with a solar-powered coffee roaster is that you need a consistent supply of sunlight to use it to run a business. The sun remains hidden for a good part of the year in the rainy Pacific Northwest, so they decided to move the business to Colorado and invited me to come with them for the adventure.

It started fine, and even fun, but slowly spun out of control. Or rather, I spun out of control. As is often the case with mental illness, I self-medicated with alcohol. All of my mental and emotional filters had self-destructed, and I had lost control of myself. My behavior became so erratic that my friends staged an intervention.

Imagine my surprise when, after an argument with the brothers, we walked into the center of town, and I found my mother standing on the sidewalk. I was going back to Georgia; I had no choice. She had my plane ticket already. They told her that if I didn't go with her peacefully, the cops were on standby. My flight left that afternoon.

I arrived back in Georgia with a single suitcase of clothing. Ten years of my life were scattered across the continent. All my other stuff — gone. Most of my relationships — dissolved. Any hope for the future — lost.

I thought my life was over.

It was.

And it wasn't.

My little sister told me, "Nate, your life is garbage. You're going to be sleeping on this couch until you figure out what God is trying to teach you. Ask Him!" At that point, it struck me as a no-lose kind of proposition. If God doesn't exist, trying to talk to Him wouldn't be any crazier than half the things I'd done in the previous two years.

But what if I was wrong?

Late one night, when I was wandering around the darkened streets of our neighborhood, I cried out to God.

"God, everything I've touched has turned to garbage. Every person I loved has thrown me away. God, if

You're real, if You exist, teach me. Teach me, Teach me, Teach me, Teach me, TEACH ME!"

. . .

God spoke.

"Stillness."

Shocked at hearing a response, I walked to the park nearby, found a bench, and tried to be still. After about 15 minutes of quiet, God spoke again.

"You danced through the pain."

I started to weep.

I knew at that moment that God is real. And He knew me.

My response to my suffering had been to try to pretend everything was ok. I drank and partied to cover up all the pain I was in all the time. Of course, it never worked.

I also suddenly knew that the Gospels are true, and that Jesus Christ is everything that I had always wanted Him to be. Messiah. Savior. Healer. The Son of God.

That night was the beginning of a whole new life.

Four days later, on Sunday, I had a vision of my parents' preacher baptizing me in a lake (They were attending a non-denominational charismatic congregation at the time). By vision, I mean VISION. I was awake with my eyes closed and it showed like a movie playing on my eyelids. It shook me tremendously because a profound sense of peace unlike any I had ever felt came with it. It was a peace that I couldn't understand.

It affected me so deeply that on Wednesday, I chimed in

during my parents' pre-meal prayer, " . . . and welcome back your prodigal son." My mom, who had been praying for my conversion for years, started jumping up and down and shouting and weeping with joy. The next day, I told her about my vision. As it turned out, the annual baptism at the nearby lake was coming up that Sunday, so seven days after I had a vision of being baptized in the lake, I was baptized in the lake. It is too miraculous for me to explain away as anything besides the hand of God.

God opened my eyes to the truth that He exists. He gave me faith. Or perhaps more accurately: He resurrected the faith that I had willingly destroyed through my sin and willful ignorance. But this faith that He gave was far beyond anything that I could have understood when I was a child. I know with complete certainty that God exists, that He knows me, and that He wants to be known by me.

In that darkened street, He also gave me hope. The knowledge of His existence is a light that pierces any darkness and drives it away. I didn't have to know what the future held, because I knew that I was being held in the palm of a loving Father. If God is for us, who can be against us?

Little did I know that I would need every scrap of faith and hope He had given me for the battle that was about to begin.

# CHAPTER 5

# Deliverance

> *These signs will accompany those who believe: in my name they will drive*
> *out demons, they will speak new languages. They will pick up serpents [with*
> *their hands], and if they drink any deadly thing, it will not harm them. They*
> *will lay hands on the sick, and they will recover."*

(LUKE 9:49-50)

THE DAY AFTER I WAS baptized in the lake, my soul vibrated like one of those paint shaking machines at the hardware store. I felt disoriented and had difficulty concentrating. In fact, I felt almost exactly like I did the day after the mental hospital released me. This time, however, I thought I knew the cause. I got on the phone: "Mom, I have a problem. I think it's demons."

"Come on over," she replied. "I know what to do about demons."

For the previous seven or eight years, my parents had studied under a charismatic preacher who regularly taught on the topic of demons and deliverance. Deliverance is prayer by any believer that aims at casting out demons. It is different from exorcism, which is a liturgical rite and sacramental that can only be practiced by a Catholic priest acting with the explicit permission of a bishop. Both have the same purpose — to cast out a demon or, in my case, many demons.

For you who are skeptical about whether my mother had the power or the authority to cast out demons, you only have to look at what Jesus said before His Ascension, "These signs will accompany those who believe: in my name they will drive out demons . . ." (MARK 16:17). He doesn't say, "These signs will accompany those who have a theology degree from a prestigious university." Nor does He say, "These signs will accompany those who have written permission from someone who ought to know better." The only qualification that God Himself asserts is faith. If you believe, this WILL happen.

And my Mom believes.

My mother was right. She did know what was wrong with me, and we began the most bizarre and extraordinary three weeks of my entire life. Casting out demon after demon.

We would start by praying and asking God to reveal what kind of demon we needed to cast out. My mom told me that sometimes she would see the name of the demon flashing like a sign above my head. Sometimes I would hear the name of a demon whispered in my heart. Sometimes I could discern the name from the nature of the powerful emotions that I was feeling –nearly uncontrollable anger accompanied a spirit of anger. Weird, I know.

Typically, the name of the demon was something like Abandonment, Murder, Fear, or Lust. In Scriptures, some demons have proper names, like Asmodeus from the book of Tobit, or Legion in the Gospels. Others are called by the name of the affliction that they cause. Jesus cast out the deaf-mute spirit by saying, "Deaf and Mute spirit, I command you to come out of him and never enter into him again" (MARK 9:25).

I don't know why, but most demons are connected to a particular sin. Because sin is part of the problem, repentance is part of the solution. So a prayer of repentance was the next step after discerning a demon's name. I would call to mind those times when I allowed the particular sin to rule over me and ask God for His forgiveness and mercy.

God's forgiveness came at a cost, though — *I* had to forgive in equal measure. Remember the Our Father, "Forgive us our trespasses as we forgive those who trespass against us." An essential part of seeking God's mercy is extending that same mercy to those who have sinned against us. I had a strong motivation to let go of my bitterness — I couldn't continue on the path to freedom with all of my grudges still holding me captive. Honestly, this was often the hardest part. I had been hurt deeply by the people closest to me.

So in prayer, I would forgive anyone who was involved in the sin I was addressing, or who had sinned against me. Forgiveness was especially important when dealing with a demon like a spirit of Abandonment. In the case of some old hurts, my anger was welded to despair. Those complicated and twisted emotions were what made me such a volcano in Colorado. This part often came with a lot of tears because it meant that I had to take out and look at all the pain I had stuffed into the dark places of my soul.

Then we would pray in tongues for a time and command the evil spirit to go. "In the name of Yeshua Bar Yahweh, I command you to go!" (That is Jesus Son of God in Hebrew.

Mom prayed like that back then, but it's not necessary. The westernized name Jesus is equally effective. )

For the biggest demons, I had to fight internal battles against them as they struggled to remain inside me. These manifested in different ways — fighting for control of my body, a torrent of violent mental imagery filling my imagination like mental pictures of cutting off my mother's head with a carving knife, emotions that surged out of nowhere to the furthest possible degree, despair that felt like it could crush me, anger that teetered on the edge of homicidal, fear so paralyzing breathing became difficult, the sensation of creatures crawling all over my body.

The sound of the command "Go" would cause me to start vomiting profusely — things I had never even eaten. Black tar-like substances, foul-tasting clear liquids, things that burned my throat and caused me to gag even more.

At the same instant, all the strong emotions and sensations would vanish as if they had never existed. I would feel something like a mild electric shock run through my body, and then I would be filled with peace, joy, and hope. So much so that I started to jump up and down and sing praises to God — just like people did when Jesus cast out demons in the Gospels.

One of the most vivid experiences started when my mother said, "Next, we have to cast out a demon called Psychopath."

Rage filled me. "You're an idiot! There's no such thing as a demon of Psychopath." Hate poured through me, and my fists balled up. Years later, my mom told me that my eyes turned completely black as I said this.

Internally, she prayed, "God, it looks like my son might try to kill me. I'm just going to keep praying." To me, she said, "Let's just try to cast it out and see if anything happens."

That seemed reasonable enough so I said, "OK," but anger still threatened to overwhelm me. When my mom commanded, "Demon of Psychopath, I command you to Go," I started coughing and then vomiting for several minutes. Super gross.

But then all of the anger vanished, to be replaced by gratitude to God, peace, and a dash of humility. "I guess you are right, Mom. That was a demon."

My thoughts and emotions became more and more peaceful as the days went on, and more and more demons fled.

My mom and I didn't work entirely alone. During this time, I was also regularly seeing a Christian counselor who was very familiar with deliverance. He has his master's in counseling from Yale and a Doctorate from Columbia Theological Seminary. He helped us to stay on track and provided a professional perspective.

I have to back up to something that I cruised past a moment ago. Prayer in tongues. Say what? Growing up Catholic, this was not a familiar concept for me, but it is apparently very common in the Pentecostal movement. It is now also common in the Catholic Charismatic Renewal.

The "gift of tongues," as St. Paul calls it, appears to come in a couple of different varieties. The first is what happened at the first Pentecost. The Holy Spirit descended upon the disciples in the upper room in the visible form of tongues of flame. The disciples then went out and spoke to the crowds, and everyone heard in their own language.

St. Paul mentions a second variety of tongues in his first letter to the Corinthians (among other places): "For one who speaks in a tongue does not speak to human beings but to God, for no one listens; he utters mysteries in spirit" (1 COR 14:2)[1].

While this kind of prayer in tongues appears to outside observers as random babble, it is not just sounds that someone makes up off the top of their head. Gibberish doesn't have any meaning whatsoever. Nor is it scat jazz singing wherein a singer strings together empty syllables and gives them pitch and meter to interweave them into the musical accompaniment. Jazz improvisation is a tremendously difficult skill to master and is the product of the human intellect.

It also shouldn't be confused with the psychotic ravings of a crazy person who jumbles words, syllables, and half-formed thoughts into a cataract of incomprehensible noise. I got very good at this form of crazy talk in the middle of my breakdown and can tell you from experience that they are very different.

My understanding is that praying in tongues is allowing God to dwell in your physical body and pray through you. God is speaking using your lips and mouth as his instrument. It is a profoundly intimate experience of God because you know that you aren't controlling what is coming out, that God is truly holding the reins. It's very peaceful and brings a profound sense of well-being and joy that God is living in me and through me and using my voice.

If this sounds crazy to you, remember that Jesus said, "When

---

1   For those who are curious about the official teaching of the Catholic Church on this phenomenon, the letter *Iuvenescit Ecclesia* from the Congregation of the Doctrine of the Faith will be very illuminating. It addresses the use of the charismatic gifts within the larger context of the institutional Church.

they hand you over, do not worry about how you are to speak or what you are to say. You will be given at that moment what you are to say. For it will not be you who speak but the Spirit of your Father speaking through you" (MATTHEW 10:19-20). If God's the one who's speaking, who am I to say that it should sound like English, German, or some angelic language that can't be understood by human beings?

It's also useful to know that prayer in tongues sounds different when practiced by different people. Whatever it sounds like, I have found it to be incredibly powerful in the context of casting out demons. To this day, if I don't know what kind of demon I'm praying against, I keep praying in tongues until God reveals something or something happens.

My first experience of praying in tongues was while trying to cast out the spirit (demon) of Pride. The demon is tenacious and powerful. It is the sin of Lucifer. So I asked my mom how we were supposed to pray it out. She responded that I would have to pray in tongues. I'd been casting out demons for over a week, so I didn't bat an eye at her answer. She took my hands in hers and started praying in tongues for a while, and asked God to bless me with the gift of praying in tongues.

We continued praying for at least another twenty minutes before I felt something welling up from within my heart. When it reached my mouth, I started speaking words and phrases, though not in any language known to me. It filled me with great peace and a feeling of the presence of God. Interiorly, it felt like being flooded with warm water. This "anointing of the Holy Spirit" filled me with the presence of Almighty God with such force that it made me feel dizzy and giggly. Charismatics call it being "drunk in the Spirit." Remember how people thought that the apostles were drunk on the day of Pentecost? That's what I'm talking about.

I felt filled with divine power. When we commanded Pride to come out, I immediately started retching and puking a foul-tasting substance — so gross, but so good. The feeling of freedom flooded through me.

If the whole process that I've described seems kind of . . . haphazard, remember that casting out demons is not like the chemical reaction where you pour vinegar onto baking soda you get a bunch of fizzing bubbles that spill all over the place. Casting out demons is a battle against spiritual beings who DO NOT WANT TO GO. Understand something very important: your soul serves them as a very comfortable home. They like it there. They will do everything in their power to stay.

So not every spiritual battle is going to look the same. To their dismay, the disciples discovered that they couldn't cast out certain demons. Jesus chastised them for their lack of faith and told them that some spirits required prayer and fasting. Like fasting, prayer in tongues is just one more tool in the arsenal against evil spirits.

I do want to respond to critics who say that prayer in tongues comes from the devil. I don't deny that you have to be careful. The devil is a copycat. One of the primary symptoms used to diagnose diabolic possession is the victim being able to speak in languages they don't know. This phenomenon mimics the gift of speaking in tongues that the Apostles received on Pentecost. Remember that the devil wants to be like God but can't. He is not creative, so he has no choice but to imitate phenomena that come from God.

I encountered the demonic equivalent to praying in tongues

sometime after my conversion. I was working as a customer service representative for the phone company. A fellow called in and told me that he wanted to block the phone number of his local prison because someone kept calling him. The guy from the prison would start gibbering into the phone the moment he answered. When the man on the phone with me imitated what he heard, the hair on my arms stood straight up and I felt the presence of something powerfully evil come upon me. The customer hung up after I blocked the prison's phone number, and I had to go to the bathroom to pray against demons for ten minutes.

You can tell the difference between the Holy Spirit's gift of prayer in tongues, the natural exercise of unstructured sound, and the demonic parody of the gift of tongues by looking at the fruit in the person's life. A person who has received the gift of tongues from God will experience good fruit in their lives: an increased desire for prayer, a love of the Scriptures and the Church, growth in virtue, repentance for sins, increased charity, and especially love for the poor. The exercise of natural ability will not affect the life of the person, although it might help book gigs in jazz clubs. The demonic version will have the opposite effects of the gift from God: disordered thinking, increased appetite for sin, and hatred for holy objects, places, and people. Exercising a demonic gift brings you into contact with demons. The more you contact you have with demons, the more power they have in your life.

During this time focused on deliverance, I realized why my mother's hands had burned my sides when I was in the middle of my breakdown. She had been quietly praying in tongues the entire time we were walking around. She listened to me rant and prayed quietly for my healing and deliverance. The demons in me burned from the power of her prayers.

From my own experience and the testimony of people involved in exorcisms, the more heavily demonized a person is, the more violently they will react against holy things. Holy water, holy oil, blessed salt, blessed rosaries, blessed crucifixes, relics of the saints . . . all these things drive demons crazy and can be used against them in the spiritual combat. When the gift of tongues comes from God, it is holy, and demons hate it.

Those three weeks of focused spiritual battle changed the way I think about the universe. Not only is God real, but so is the devil. And he wasn't about to let me go without a fight. Satan had invested too much time and energy leading me down the wide road that leads to destruction. The war for my soul was just beginning. This was just the opening battle.

# CHAPTER 6

# Cleanse your hands

*So submit yourselves to God. Resist the devil, and he will flee from you. Draw near to God, and he will draw near to you. Cleanse your hands, you sinners, and purify your hearts, you of two minds. Begin to lament, to mourn, to weep. Let your laughter be turned into mourning and your joy into dejection. Humble yourselves before the Lord and he will exalt you.*

(JAMES 4:7-10)

THOSE THREE WEEKS OF spiritual detox were a turning point in my life, but that wasn't the end of my battle with the devil. I had spent the previous decade, maybe longer, going my own way. The devil's way. The wide and easy road to perdition.

Submitting myself to God had not even made it to the bottom of my to-do list in all that time. It would not now come easily. God needed to get rid of a lot of my bad habits.

To submit to God, I needed to know what He wants. The ordinary way that He speaks to us is through the Scriptures and the Church. But Jesus also promised, "when he comes, the Spirit of Truth, he will guide you to all truth. He will not speak on his own, but he will speak what he hears, and will declare to you the things that are coming. He will glorify me, because he will take from what is mine and declare it to you." (JOHN 16:13-14)

The voice I heard in the dark of night was the Spirit of Truth. The Holy Spirit — and I wanted more. Knowing that God could speak made me hungry to hear from Him again.

God is eager to speak to us, but we need to cultivate silence. The witness of the Church, the Scriptures, and the lives of the Saints tells us that God desires a direct, personal relationship with His people. A relationship includes speaking to them one on one.

At first, it was very difficult for me to quiet myself enough to hear the voice of God clearly. I asked Him to speak more loudly. He said, "No." Then I discovered that I could hear that still, small voice say "yes" and "no" pretty clearly if I took the time to stop whatever I was doing and pay attention.

I would go on prayer walks through my parent's neighborhood. At every intersection, I would pray and ask the Lord if He wanted me to go left, right, or straight. I would listen for the yes, and then go in that direction. I sometimes did this for hours. I bought some Chaco sandals to protect the soles of my feet. My parents' neighborhood was big enough that I never quite explored it completely or got to know the layout. Right around the time I started to get tired or thirsty, I would find myself on familiar streets near their house.

I decided to apply this practice to my employment situation. I had debts I needed to pay, a dwindling bank account, and no income. I asked the Lord if I should start looking for a job. It was August. "No, pray," was God's response. I asked again in

September, October, and November and heard the same thing. I was starting to get a little worried. Yet I trusted that God had some way of finding me a job when I needed one. "Seek ye first the kingdom of God, and all these things shall be added unto you," and all that.

December came along, and I was down to my very last dollars, an empty bank account and maxed out credit cards. I asked again if I could start looking for a job, and He said, "Yes." I found two job openings and sent in my resume to both. I got two interviews. I landed the first job right away and started working a week later. God's timing is always perfect. A month later, I got the second job, which doubled my salary and gave me health benefits. God knew exactly what He was doing.

The second job was perfect for me, but not in the way that you might imagine. I got hired as a customer service representative for the phone company. Whenever someone wanted to yell at the phone company, they would call me. I tried to solve their problem and then sell them new phone products. Like $5 voicemail. Just about the hardest sales job imaginable.

I had (have) a temper problem; it's like a fiery inferno. I have put holes in walls and doors more than once. It's part of the reason that my fiancé broke up with me via a restraining order, and my friends in Colorado staged an intervention. Anger had me by the throat.

My new job required me to talk to angry people all day long (and sometimes with mandatory overtime). For three years, my job was to talk to ten thousand angry people a year and not lose my temper. God has a sense of humor.

During this time, I got a plantar wart on my big toe. One of those big ones that grow and grow and grow. I wanted to get rid of it, but when I prayed about it, the Lord said, "No." I left it alone for a couple of months. I was kind of hoping that He'd heal it miraculously. Instead, it got bigger and bigger, and new warts started forming in the general area. And it started to hurt. I prayed about it again. Again, God said, "No." The wart became uncomfortable, then painful, until I started to have trouble walking. Every step that I took caused pain to shoot up my leg.

Six or seven months later, I asked the Lord if I could PLEASE get the wart removed, and He said, "Yes." I went to a dermatologist, and she said she would have to freeze it off with liquid nitrogen. Unfortunately, it had grown to about the size of a dime so that it would take multiple treatments over a couple of months. In between treatments, I had to scrub away the dead skin with a pumice stone every time I took a shower.

The pain of scrubbing that stupid wart took my breath away. It was worse than when I was walking around on it. I persisted, and after more than a month of rasping away, the main wart and all the little tiny warts vanished as well. I was so relieved.

Why did I have to go through all that? I was perplexed. After the trial, God told me that the effect of that wart on my foot was like the effect of my uncontrollable anger on my soul. Even if I tried to ignore it, anger was a constant and growing source of suffering for me and for those around me. The remedy for that spiritual wart was a good, hard, painful cleansing. The phone company and that multitude of angry people acted like a spiritual pumice stone grinding away at the infected tissue in my soul.

Once the devil leads us to develop sinful habits like my anger, most of his work is done. He can sit back and relax. The sinful habits take on a life of their own like a plantar wart burrowing into the skin. Breaking those habits is hard, painful, and in fact impossible without God's grace. We cannot save ourselves from sin through human effort. God lead me to the phone company because it was a cross that was perfectly tailored to help remove the sin of uncontrollable anger from my life.

While working for the phone company, I returned to the Catholic Church. One day, God told me, "Nathan, you're Catholic." My response was, "Oh, that's right. I'm Catholic." I asked a friend what I needed to do to return to the Catholic Church and learned that, since I had already received the sacraments of baptism, communion, and confirmation, the only requirement was to go to confession. I immediately called the local parish and told the priest that I needed the sacrament of confession. When he responded with the weekly confession schedule, I retorted, "I'm coming back to the Church after ten years of apostasy and living like a heathen. I'm going to need more time than that." He very graciously scheduled an appointment for later that week.

Confession took about an hour the first time around. I felt GREAT afterward. Renewed. Reborn. Resurrected. I didn't understand this at the time, but the sacrament of confession is filled with divine power. Through it, God forgives our sins. But He doesn't stop there. He also heals our souls of the effects of sin and gives us the grace that we need to resist sin in the future. If the phone company was my pumice stone, confession was God's liquid nitrogen, killing sin at the root.

Regular confession is one of the most powerful means we have for resisting the devil. Sin is the devil's most powerful weapon against us, and repentance is our most powerful defense.

God's forgiveness destroys the shackles of sin. He taught me this lesson in a most dramatic fashion.

I woke with a start one night. I lay there for a little while feeling dazed and a little bit annoyed. I felt like I had woken up for some REASON, but I had no idea what it could be. I asked God if He wanted to tell me anything.

"I'm going to make you hungry for humility and purity," He said. Then He poked me in the chest. A radiant delight flooded through me like nothing I've ever experienced in my entire life. The total unexpectedness of that moment is frozen in my memory. It hasn't happened since.

At that moment, God changed something in me. He planted seeds of desire for humility and purity. A new hunger. Not only did I know that I needed to change some things about myself, but I now had the desire to take up the struggle.

Some time later, God sat me down for a little 'chat.' He said that He wasn't preparing me to marry some random woman. He was preparing me to marry His daughter. He told me that protecting the purity of the relationship was going to be my responsibility and that failure to do so would be catastrophic.

I asked Him what He meant by catastrophic. He responded, "Adam and Eve. David and Bathsheba. Catastrophic!" I don't know if you have ever had a parent or teacher scare the stupid out of you by warning you of the consequences of your actions. I can tell you with absolute certainty that no one can instill the Fear of God better than God Himself. I know to this day that I never want to know what He meant when He said, "Catastrophic!"

I had to deal with the problem of purity, specifically the problem of sexual purity.

I'm going to talk about some real sins here, so if you have already mastered sexual purity, you might want to skip to page 52, because you might find it gross. All sin is gross, but sexual sin is particularly gross. I'll do my best to keep it PG. PG-13, maybe.

\* \* \*

This page intentionally left blank

Like 99.9% of modern men, I believed that masturbation was not only good but practically a medical necessity. This belief stands directly opposed to the perennial teaching of the Church that it is a mortal sin and will lead you straight to hell. Where does the Church get this seemingly backward idea? Hmmmmmm. Oh, that's right, from God.

> "You have heard that it was said, 'You shall not commit adultery.' But I say to you, everyone who looks at a woman with lust has already committed adultery with her in his heart. If your right eye causes you to sin, tear it out and throw it away. It is better for you to lose one of your members than to have your whole body thrown into Gehenna. And if your right hand causes you to sin, cut it off and throw it away. It is better for you to lose one of your members than to have your whole body go into Gehenna."
> (MATTHEW 5:27-30)

I want you to notice something. First, Jesus says that if you look at a woman with lust in your heart that you've committed adultery with her in your heart. With His next breath, He says that you should gouge out your eye or cut off your hand if it is causing you to sin. I don't think He could more explicitly refer to the abuse of pornography or masturbation if He tried. The penalty for these sins? To be cast into the fires of hell.

Why is this sin such a big deal? Isn't it harmless? Isn't God just spoiling our fun by making this activity off-limits? That's what the devil would like you to think.

Love and lust are opposed to one another. When I love someone, I want what's best for them. If I lust after somebody, I want to use that other person in a way that is pleasurable to me. Masturbation is an act of pure lust. Another person becomes a sex toy in the sinner's imagination, performing who knows what kinds of degrading and dehumanizing acts. Taking delight in evil like this isn't good for us, spiritually, mentally, or emotionally.

There also happens to be lots of big, nasty demons connected with lust. When you commit sins of lust, you're building a nice comfortable nest for them to call home. They're more than happy to move in and take over.

Jesus tries to tell us that sexual purity is serious business. In that passage, He basically says that the abuse of pornography and masturbation are the exact same thing as adultery. That may be part of the reason that it is so destructive to marriages.

St. Paul clarifies further when he talks about the lust of the eye and the lust of the flesh. I was fighting two different but interconnected types of lust.

Lust of the eye refers to the desire to view sexualized beauty. Brain science tells us that sexual imagery lights up the brain in very specific ways that pictures of puppies or your grandmother do not (or should not). This desire is different from the lust of the flesh, which is the desire for physical pleasure (Jesus's reference to the hand). The two kinds of lust are strongly connected, and the connection grows through years of practice, but they are still two very different things. Knowing you are fighting two different battles makes a big difference.

I had a little bit of an advantage in the lust of the eye department. Right after my conversion, I had a horrifying experience that forever cured me of my desire to look at pornography. I turned on the computer and pulled up a porn site. Immediately, I noticed a sensation like bugs crawling up my arms. I tried to ignore it, but it increased rapidly and freaked me out. It was the sensation of little demons crawling up my arms toward my head.

I turned off the computer and started doing deliverance prayer, but the sensation continued for several minutes before going away completely. Think about it. It makes sense. The pornography business is wicked. Fed by drugs, human trafficking, greed, and lust. There's no doubt the devil has his hand in it. Big time.

I then had the realization that in an unknown percentage of pornographic videos, I was not just watching sex acts but rapes. Human trafficking provides vast numbers of women who are forced to participate in pornography through drug use, captivity, and violence. By abusing pornography, I was enriching their captors and in a very real way contributing to their misery and even their deaths. The life expectancy of women captured by human traffickers is notoriously short. God have mercy on me. Just thinking about it now makes me feel a little sick.

Lust of the flesh didn't want to go quietly. When I decided to stop masturbating forever, the devil fought back like an angry wildcat. I hallucinated naked women floating over my bed. I could feel disembodied hands touching me all over, stirring up sexual arousal. The spirit of lust used my memory of pornographic images and sinful sexual experiences as a weapon against me by constantly bringing them to mind. My emotions and desires raged uncontrollably. I would become sexually aroused at the most random times. It was the first time in my life that I recognized that I was truly a slave to sin.

I kept losing the battle to cleanse my hands. The Holy Spirit inspired me to stop putting so much trust in myself and start putting more trust in grace. On the advice of my spiritual director (you'll meet him in the next chapter), I decided to go to confession every time that I fell into sexual sin. It was embarrassing and humiliating, but I needed the grace of God's forgiveness to be able to keep up the battle.

The battle raged for months, and the devil was not giving up. Once he has you ensnared in sexual sin, he will do everything in his power to keep you in the trap. Without grace, it is impossible to escape. I needed to be saved from my sin. I was not only battling a habitual sin but a very real addiction to chemicals produced in my brain by my bad behavior. I nearly despaired of ever being freed.

Then one day, God did it. He saved me from my sin. One morning, the power and attraction of the devil's temptations dropped from 10.5 on a 10-point scale to something like a 1.2. I still occasionally have moments when the devil tries to tempt me to sexual sin (I have to walk to the other side of the mall when I go past a Victoria's Secret), but I can tell him to flee in the name of Jesus, and the temptation comes to an end.

I also learned that the physical feeling of pressure, the "I'm going to explode" feeling that comes from a period of sexual arousal that is not followed by an orgasm, eventually goes away. Any build-up of seminal fluid flows out during urination after the arousal passes. I learned to embrace the discomfort of feeling the need for sexual release. Not sinning would not kill me but continuing to sin would kill me eternally. I also learned to avoid things that caused sexual arousal inappropriately, also known as the "near occasion of sin." That's why I steer clear of lingerie stores.

Years have now passed since I last committed the sins of viewing pornography or masturbating. At the time of the battle, I thought it was impossible. Now I look back, and I'm so grateful that God carried me through. Purity is freedom.

\* \* \*

God wanted to reward me for my victory in this battle. Shortly afterward, I went into work one Monday morning and discovered that I had Thursday and Friday off. The phone company did this weird thing where I had to schedule all my vacation days a year in advance. A four-day weekend sounded awesome, so I asked God what He wanted me to do with the time. He told me, "Go camping." I had not been camping in about ten years, but I thought it sounded great. I did some research and found a campground about three hours away.

I planned a very simple trip, with only peanut butter and jelly sandwiches for meals, and I decided to go alone so that I could get some good quiet time with the Lord. On Friday morning, I hopped into my car and drove north toward the campground. At around 11:00, I arrived at my destination but discovered to my horror that the campground was closed. For renovations. Until January. Giant piles of sand were scattered all over the campground, and everything was torn to pieces. I sat in my car and prayed, "God, You wanted me to go camping, but apparently not here. Where to?"

I looked at a map that I had downloaded onto my phone and picked a place that was about 25 minutes away. When I got there, it was terrible. As I drove through, a fat shirtless redneck eyeballed me from behind his campfire with a scowl on his face. The only spot left was next to the porta-potties. I told Jesus, "NO, this is not Your plan. This place is terrible. I'm going to keep driving." I pulled back onto the highway with no clue where I was going.

I drove for about an hour through the Georgia mountains, past several campsites to which God responded, "No," when asked if He wanted me to camp there. At one point, I got frustrated and angry, so I stopped at an overlook and prayed, "God, I'm not moving another inch until You give me some peace that You've got this under control." As I sat looking over the Smoky Mountains, I pulled out the Mass readings for the day. The Gospel reading came from Matthew 12:43-45, the one about the demon who is cast out, wanders in the desert, and returns to his former home with seven of his evil friends to retake the soul that it had lost.

God helped me to see that this was what was going on. When I was an atheist, faithlessness and unbelief were two demons that ruled my life. I kicked them out after my conversion, but they had come back to try to take over again. Suddenly it made sense: God was testing my faith with this journey. Was I going to trust Him, or listen to the demons who were telling me that what I was doing was crazy? Peace flooded in, I hopped back into my car and took to the open road. I drove for about another three hours through the Georgia mountains, with absolutely no idea where I was going. It was a beautiful day. I love driving in the mountains. I told God, "I LOVE driving in the mountains!" He responded, "I know. It is part of the plan."

Eventually, God told me to pull into a campground at a place called Desoto Falls, in the shadow of Blood Mountain. I had called them earlier in the week and they said they were full, but now they had one spot available. The place was beautiful. A stream flowed through the site, and two waterfalls were within walking distance of my tent.

I pitched my tent and hiked to one of the waterfalls to pray. As I walked, I passed a family with two little girls. The mom was telling them a story about Jesus and some orphans. I smiled and waved as I walked past, but I was moving more quickly than they were, so I got to the waterfall about 10 minutes before they did. As they walked up, I asked one of the girls, "So y'all like stories about Jesus?" It was a great way to start the conversation. The couple worked as youth ministers at a Presbyterian church south of Atlanta. They enjoyed what they were doing, but their hearts were really in the charismatic movement, specifically as it relates to discipleship and building community.

We had a great conversation, and they invited me to come to their camp and eat chili and smores with them. We ended up talking until late that night, praying and studying Scripture together. The Lord spoke to us very simply about faith and what it means to live the life of faith.

The life of faith consists of hearing what the Lord wants and then doing it. Even if that means driving through the mountains for hours when you have no idea where you will sleep, without knowing that God will have chili and smores waiting for you when you get there. It's simple to say but very difficult to do. You have to learn to hear and recognize when God is speaking to you, then trust Him enough to obey His commands. "Be a doer of the Word and not a hearer only." (JAMES 1:22)

The family invited me back for breakfast the next morning, and again the conversation was delightful. We decided to part ways for the afternoon and meet up again for dinner. That night we sat around the campfire and discussed spiritual warfare — one of my favorite topics. We stayed up late into the night, praying together again. The next morning, we ate breakfast together and chatted before praying and parting ways.

On the way home, I marveled at God's goodness. All He said was, "Go camping," but that simple instruction contained an adventure beyond my wildest imaginings.

Learning to submit yourself to God and be cleansed of your sins is challenging. You have to pay attention to what He's saying to you, whether He's speaking to you directly in prayer, or through a counselor like a spiritual director, or the teachings of His Church. Listening is not enough; you have to obey. The Lord's leading is fruitless if you don't follow.

# CHAPTER 7

# Coming to Community

*They devoted themselves to the teaching of the apostles and to the communal life, to the breaking of the bread and to prayers. Awe came upon everyone, and many wonders and signs were done through the apostles.*

(ACTS 3:42-43)

IN THE MONTHS FOLLOWING my conversion, Jesus and demons were pretty much all that I talked about to anyone who would listen. Even to people who were not particularly interested in listening. I discovered that my old friends from Hollywood largely fit in the second category. One friend told me that my new beliefs were too dogmatic and closeminded for his tastes, so he disinvited me to his wedding and ended our friendship. In his defense, I am a pretty exuberant person, especially when it comes to my conversion.

The Lord had other plans and other friends in store. I live in the Bible Belt, so talking about Jesus and God's awesomeness is generally well received. When I shared my testimony with a coworker at my new job, she told me, "You should check out the Alleluia Community. I think they'll understand you." She was right. Her name happened to be Aletheia, which means "truth" in Greek.

The Alleluia Community started in 1972 when a group of families decided that they wanted to live communally in the way early Christians did as described in the book of Acts. The founders were Catholics who had experienced the Charismatic Renewal, which focuses on the baptism and indwelling of the Holy Spirit. Through the Charismatic Renewal, they had discovered prayer in tongues, deliverance from evil spirits, and the power gifts like prophecy, healing and miracles.

The community initially held everything in common like the early disciples did, putting all of their paychecks into a common fund, donating their cars into a sharing pool, picking up and leaving their old lives behind to try to follow Jesus with every ounce of their energy. When the community was first founded, it admittedly had some similarities with the hippie communes that were popular at the time, with the important distinction of rejecting the drug use and sexual promiscuity that characterized the flower children. They were "mustard seed" children instead.

The community is ecumenical, and it's not a church in itself. Most of the members are Catholic (including several diocesan priests and permanent deacons), but the community also has Lutherans, Anglicans, Methodists, Pentecostals, and members of other New Charismatic Churches. The members have agreed not to try to proselytize members from other denominations. The key insight of Alleluia's life is that division among Christians is not primarily caused by a failure of doctrine but rather by a refusal to love one another. Unity is impossible without love.

Disagreements can and do arise in the community about all kinds of things, including matters of faith, but the commitment to love one another is the source of Alleluia's remarkable unity.

By the time I showed up on the scene, Alleluia had been around for nearly 40 years. It had grown from the original five families to more than 800 members. They run a private K-12 school and have transformed a once-blighted neighborhood into an oasis they call Faith Village, which became my home. My coworker introduced me to someone who grew up inside the community. More invitations followed, and I started to get to know more of the members.

The event that made me think, "I belong here," was something that Alleluia calls "Work Party." One Saturday a month, fathers and sons in the community meet at the Alleluia Community School. They start with prayer, singing praise and worship — sometimes have breakfast — and then work on the school for the next 3-4 hours. I saw guys doing everything from cutting the grass to plumbing to tearing down walls. It is their school, and they act on their responsibility to take care of it.

The members have a remarkable faith borne from their experiences of God's action in their lives. My stories of insanity and deliverance didn't raise any eyebrows. Anyone who listened to one would laugh and top my story with one that would curl my hair. God had gone to extraordinary lengths to bring this group of people together, and their stories proved it. They have plenty of experience with casting out demons and have worked with the diocesan exorcist when needed.

I wanted very badly to move out of my parent's house and into Faith Village, but it wasn't quite time yet. God was moving around the pieces. On Independence Day, I went to the July 4th festivities in Center Circle, which is a block of houses that surrounds a giant shared backyard. I wandered into a house to use the bathroom and started a conversation that would change my life forever.

Mike Firmin moved from Louisiana to join Alleluia Community in the early '80s. A lifelong servant of the poor, Mike was approached by a community action group to start a food bank for Augusta. In 1982, Mike founded the nonprofit that would come to be known as Golden Harvest Food Bank. Over the next 30 years, he would grow the ministry to serve 30 counties in Georgia and South Carolina, feeding the hungry in partnership with a network of more than 500 hunger relief agencies.

During my conversation with Mike, I shared my testimony and mentioned my desire to move to Faith Village. Much to my surprise, he offered me a room in his house. It is not uncommon for members of Alleluia to do something called "household." In household, a person who is interested in the Community will move in with a family and share life with them. It's a great way to build relationships and find out if God wants the household member to join the community.

I got Mike's phone number, and within a couple of days, we agreed that I would move into his house after his son got married and moved out in a few months. Thus began the most transformative period of my Christian life so far: discipleship.

I say without reservation that Mike is a spiritual super-ninja, and he became my spiritual director. I still call him Yoda, which he thinks is funny.

If you look at the Gospels and the history of the Church, the faith doesn't typically appear out of nowhere. It is handed down from person to person. Jesus taught His disciples this way, and they handed it on to another generation of disciples, on and on through the ages until our present day. If there's any similarity between the path of Christian discipleship and the training that a Padawan receives from a Jedi Knight, it's because Christians have been passing down invaluable wisdom this way for millennia.

After I moved into Mike's house, he began the difficult work of teaching me spiritual discipline. One day he said, "I think that you need to start to get up in the morning to pray." My job at the phone company didn't start until 10 A.M. so I regularly slept until 8-8:30.

"So, what do you think," I replied, "7-7:30?"

"You should get up with me at 5:00."

I was nonplussed, but I had agreed to allow Mike to train me in the spiritual life. So, I moved my bedtime from 1:00 am to 10:00 PM and started to get up at 5:00 in the morning to pray. It took a while to get used to it because I had deliberately cultivated a night owl lifestyle since middle school. Slowly but surely, I adjusted to the change.

Spending two hours a day in prayer and meditation on the Bible will change your life. Mike knew this from long experience, so he was able to transmit it to me. It was a question of obedience for me, though. More than once, I was tempted with the rebellious thought, "I am a grown man. Am I going to let this guy give me a bedtime?" The practice of daily prayer became deeply ingrained in me, and it's a discipline that I continue a decade later without supervision. I took ownership of it.

He also hosted a weekly men's Bible study focused on the practice of Lectio Divina. Lectio Divina is Latin for "sacred reading" and has a history that goes back more than a thousand years. The foundation for Lectio is the belief that the Sacred Scriptures are holy and inspired by God. They contain layers of meaning hidden from a casual reader. God can speak to the reader who approaches the Bible prayerfully.

Lectio Divina has been described in detail by great saints, but here is what it looked like during our Bible study. We started every session with a prayer to the Holy Spirit to open God's Word to us and to open our hearts to understand. Then one person would read a short passage from the book that we were studying. Then we would have a few moments of silence so that we could listen to what God wanted to say to us through the Scriptures. When it felt appropriate, someone would start to share any insights that came to mind. After a few minutes of discussion, someone would read the next passage, and the process would repeat.

We stopped after an hour and went around the room, and each man shared his prayer intentions. The group would pray for each man in turn. In some ways, the prayers were the most powerful part of the Bible study because I saw prayers answered. Sometimes not immediately, but I did the Bible study weekly for years, and the fruit of the study and the prayers was very apparent.

Perhaps the biggest impact of my 'household' experience came from my regular spiritual direction meetings with Mike. They were nothing formal, just regular half-hour to hour long conversations about what was going on in my spiritual life. It was in these meetings that I learned a little something called "discernment." Discernment is super important.

Not every thought or feeling or desire comes from the Lord. Nor does every temptation come from the devil. These movements of the mind, will, and emotions come from one of four sources: the internal, the external, the eternal, or the infernal. God can and does speak to us, but we don't always recognize it at the time. It becomes especially difficult when strong emotions are involved.

The internal sources are your thoughts, desires, and emotions. Unfortunately, these internal sources are not perfect and don't always lead us to the good, the true, and the beautiful. The Fall added concupiscence — the darkness of the mind, weakness of the will, and disorder in the emotions — to the mix, so our thoughts, feelings, and emotions are not always reliable guides. Matters get more complicated because our actions can become habits of thought and feeling over time. Unfortunately, bad habits carry the same or even more weight in our internal life as good habits. Mental illness and emotional trauma can also dramatically affect our thoughts, desires, and emotions. Our emotions are not trustworthy if our neurotransmitters are out of whack. So, internal sources are a mix of true and untrue.

The external sources are likewise a mix. These are all the inputs that you receive each day through your senses: the music that you listen to, the videos that you watch, the books that you read, the people that you talk to, the organizations that you support. If you're careful about what kinds of media you consume, it can build you up.[1] But unfettered access to media can be quite destructive. I haven't owned a television for more than

---

1    I really loved reading the encyclicals of Pope Leo XIII. He's both a philosophical ninja and a mystic. He wrote the St. Michael the Archangel prayer after hearing a conversation between Jesus and the devil as he processed to the altar.

a decade because I realized that nearly everything I watched tempted me to sin. Lust, greed, envy, doubt. Name a sin, and you can find a channel that caters to it. I also had to destroy my entire pre-conversion music collection because nearly all my favorite songs had some connection to the sins of the past.

The eternal sources always lead us towards the good. God can speak to us directly, appear in visions, enkindle images in our imagination, or stir up holy desires. He also uses other agents, which include the saints (the Blessed Mother in particular), angels (Gabriel, our guardian angels), the sacred Scriptures, the Sacred Tradition, the sacraments, and righteous authority (like good spiritual direction). God wants what's good for us, so He constantly tries to reach us with His core message — repent and believe the Gospel. He also promises in the Scriptures that the Holy Spirit will lead us into all truth.

The infernal sources are, in fact, diabolical. The enemy of human nature is constantly at work, trying to lead us into sin. He can penetrate our defenses through our senses, our thoughts, our desires, our imagination, false logic, and disordered relationships. The goal of the evil one is simple: to lead us away from God into the abyss of hell, where we will suffer eternal punishment with him. One of the great falsehoods of the Satanists is that hell is Satan's kingdom. It's not. It's his prison. God reigns over hell the same way He reigns over everything else. Every message that comes from an infernal source is false and leads to misery and sorrow, even if if the results seem temporarily fun. Satan loves to trap us with things that are fun but not good.

The difficulty in discernment comes from untangling these four channels so we can tune into the eternal. Human beings are easily deceived. Bias often clouds our thinking, so we choose to believe what we *WANT* to believe rather than what is true.

For instance, I can think of three times that I thought that God wanted me to marry some woman who had caught my eye. I was wrong every time. Mike was there to pray through it with me and encourage me to exercise restraint. As a result, I didn't make an idiot of myself by going up to these women and saying, "I think God wants us to get married." I did still FEEL like an idiot, especially as I watched each of them walk down the aisle toward some other guy wearing a tuxedo, but at least they didn't have to know about it.

Poor discernment can also have tragic consequences. My best friend during this time was Brian. He was a former seminarian who came to the community when he realized that he was not supposed to be a priest. He was very intelligent, had studied theology for years, and loved to debate. We had a great time arguing about faith. I heard "Nathan, you're wrong" more than once, and often (but not always), he was correct.

As we got close over the years, I learned that he had also suffered some pretty serious mental, emotional, and even physical abuse when he was growing up. That kind of abuse can leave deep scars, which can come to the surface through mental illnesses like depression, PTSD, disassociation, etc.

I knew that Brian was going through a rough patch, but I didn't realize how dark it was getting for him internally. He didn't tell me what was going on. He enrolled in technical training to get a job as some type of medical technician.

"Brian is dead."

When I got the text message, my heart nearly stopped. I was at work, and I think I just hung up on the customer that

I had on the line. I hardly remember anything besides the devastation that I felt when I read those words. I left work and went home, where I just collapsed on the floor, weeping. I later went to the adoration chapel and spent several hours weeping prostrate before the Blessed Sacrament.

Suicide leaves a hole in your life that is impossible to understand. The person should be there, but they suddenly aren't. Depression and despair lead Brian to kill himself. He thought that he had failed his final exams and that the door to his chosen career path had closed. A couple of weeks after his death, a letter came from the training program — an acceptance letter.

The evil one used Brian's emotional instability to push him over the edge. When depression brings you to the brink, it doesn't take much to cover the distance that remains. If he'd been more discerning, he would have realized that his despair was deeply irrational and that it didn't fit with the eternal perspective. God was going to take care of him, whether he got into the program or not. In the heat of the emotional struggle, Brian lost sight of this truth and then lost the battle.

For months, I cried every day. I was so sad. Mike gave me the book 'Searching for and Maintaining Peace' by Fr. Jacques Phillipe. I started going to the perpetual adoration chapel almost every night, where I would read a couple of pages, pray for a while, and then rest. This time of healing sparked my love of Eucharistic adoration, which continues to this day.

Time doesn't heal all wounds, but the scar tissue does get less sensitive. I will always regret losing Brian. Would he have found "the one," gotten married, and had children? What kind of adventures would we have shared? One moment of despair obliterated the answers to those questions. It makes me think about my moment at the brink of death, on top of my sister's apartment building in the tar pits. How much life would I have missed if I had given in to the chaos inside? What tremendous mercy that God chose to give me a second chance!

Slowly the pain ebbed away. Life continued.

While living with Mike, he introduced me to something called Theophostic Prayer ministry. It comes from the Greek words meaning God (Theos) and light (phos). The idea behind Theophostic prayer ministry is that God can shine His light into our painful memories and bring about remarkable emotional healings.

It helps to do this with someone experienced in the practice, especially if you have never done it before. After you have some experience with it, you can do it privately during a time of prayer. I have experienced a lot of healing this way over the years.

You start with a prayer asking God to bring light and healing to your memories. You'll probably start with a specific memory in mind, or the Holy Spirit might call one to your attention after you begin. Often these memories come from some of the most painful times of your life, which is one of the reasons why it is good to do it with a trusted and experienced person.

You imagine yourself to be in the memory, and then you ask God to reveal where He was during the painful experience. Then you wait for the Holy Spirit to reveal something to you. When you pray in faith, expecting God to do something, it's truly remarkable what He does.

One of my most powerful experiences of Theophostic ministry focused on my nervous breakdown. Obviously, it was the most destructive and chaotic episode in my entire life. Where was God when I ran naked through the streets of Los Angeles?

After opening with prayer, I closed my eyes and imagined the street where it took place. The lawns were perfectly kept, bathed in the sickly yellow light from streetlights. I saw myself naked on the lawn, covered with demons. A surging mass of black creatures devoured me. I asked God to show me where He was in all this darkness.

Suddenly, in my imagination, Jesus appeared with a lightsaber in His hand. Demons scattered at His approach but the minute He turned His back, would swarm in from the other side. The battle raged for a few seconds, and then my memory faded to black.

Then I recalled the quiet voice that I heard that night, so different from all the others. The one that suggested that I go onto the lawn instead of crushing my skull against the asphalt. I realized that He'd been there. Pushing me back from the edge of the abyss.

I wept for a long time but felt refreshed when I finished. Renewed. Resurrected. Ready for something different.

It was a good thing, because something different was coming.

After three years of working my terrible job at the phone company that I hated with all my heart and living with Mike, he and I met for one of our regular spiritual direction sessions. I was thinking about applying for a promotion to supervisor, which would mean that I would only get to talk to the most angry, frustrated, and nasty customers — the ones who demanded to speak to a supervisor. Mike looked at me quietly for at least a minute. I was used to that. It meant he was praying about something.

"I think the Holy Spirit wants you to be the new grant writer for the food bank," he finally said. I looked at him with that kind of tilt-headed expression that dogs use when they don't understand what's going on. I had never written a grant in my entire life. When I told him that, he responded, "Pray about it." It was Holy Week, so I said we could talk about it after Easter. I asked him how much the job paid, and he answered that it was about $8,000 less than I was making at the phone company. I told him that I would pay $8,000 a year to never talk about phone bills again.

Never one to let moss grow on a rock, Mike arranged for me to meet with the Associate Director of the Food Bank the next day. Barry Forde, God rest his soul, spent nearly 30 years at the Food Bank, and belonged to Alleluia. He spoke glowingly of the call to serve the poor and how acting on God's call to feed the hungry had transformed his life. After talking for two hours, he suggested that I meet Mike's successor, who had been training under Mike for two years and would take over in a year when Mike retired. I said, "Sure." Barry called the next day and scheduled a meeting for the morning of Holy Thursday.

When I met with Mike's successor, I told him, "If you offer me this job, I'll take it, because it's crazy for you to offer me this job. Only the Holy Spirit could make this happen." He offered me the job on the spot, and I took it, pay cut and all.

I went into the phone company and told my boss that I had taken another job. She was disappointed to lose me but delighted by the opportunity that God had given me. She told me that I could work the next day, and then she would put me on vacation until my saved-up days off were paid out. She didn't want me to worry about giving two weeks' notice, though she appreciated the fact that I offered to stay.

My last day at the phone company was Good Friday. That

day, I put down this particular cross. I was in a great mood as I talked to my customers. My last call came in at 5:55 P.M. The caller's name?

Trinity.

# CHAPTER 8

# Dealing with the occult

*"... a charming mistress of witchcraft, who enslaved nations with her prostitution, and peoples by her witchcraft: I now come against you — oracle of the Lord of hosts"*

(NAHUM 3:4-5)

TELLING STORIES OF MY battles with the devil always gives me a thrill. Remember, I have a degree in theater. Give me an audience and a story to tell, and I'm the happiest man alive. One day, a good friend of mine invited me to share my conversion testimony with his high school youth group. He's a hilarious guy who loves Jesus and is always trying to figure out ways to make the faith real to young people. Battles with the devil are about as real as it gets.

So, we set up a time for me to eat pizza with them and share my testimony. My friend's parish has an active youth group, with 45-50 young men who show up regularly for the meetings. On the day of the talk, my buddy called up and said, "Dude, we have a problem. One of my guys just called me and told me that he was playing with a Ouija board, and the demon manifested. He's totally freaked out. Can we do some deliverance on him tonight?"

"Of course!" I replied. "Casting out demons is my favorite thing in the world. No problem." I got pretty pumped, even though this was pretty foolish in retrospect. I've since learned to respect the devil as an enemy. If I got the same phone call today, the following would never have happened.

When we got to the meeting, my pal started us out with prayer and then allowed the young man who played with the Ouija Board to tell his story. Fascination with evil is one of the devil's snares, and he had caught this kid. I could tell that the episode freaked him out a little, but he clearly enjoyed sharing a story that so obviously terrified the other kids. Causing fear feels powerful.

I could tell the boy had been dabbling with the occult for a while because he knew too much about it. He told how they set up the board and summoned a spirit, which began speaking to them through the planchette (the little piece of wood with a hole in it that points to the letters on the Ouija board). He asked the demon its number, which apparently signifies its importance in the legions of hell. That he knew to ask the demon this question showed me that this was not his first time summoning demons. He said that an evil presence filled the room, and everyone freaked out, especially when it wouldn't leave when they tried to command it. They decided to get rid of the board entirely by throwing it into the river. When it hit the water, they heard a blood-curdling scream.

At this point, all the boys in the room look terrified, I'm slightly miffed at the young man's idiocy, and the young man looks downright happy that he's scared all the kids at the youth ministry. My friend said, "Wow. That's terrible. So now I want to introduce you to my buddy, Nathan."

I started by telling them a little bit about my story and how I had to cast a whole bunch of demons out of myself because of my contact with the occult. I explained that divination, or summoning demons to get special knowledge, was a mortal sin and opened one's soul to demonic infestation and possession. Even touching items like tarot cards, Ouija boards, or other tools of divination could open the door for demons to attack.

I explained that I was going to cast out the demon that had attacked this young man because the name of Jesus was all-powerful, and the demon would have to leave.

When I started to pray in tongues, the young man's head dropped down to his chest. I stopped and asked him what was going on, but he didn't respond. He seemed completely coma-tose. Some of the other young men in the room got up and left because the immediate change in the young man frightened them so much. One of the boys later said that he got a pounding headache the moment I started to pray.

"Lord Jesus, please help me do what I'm supposed to do here," I silently prayed. I had a vision in my imagination of the demon manifesting through the boy, so I silently prayed, "Demon, I bind you in the name of Jesus Christ. I command you not to manifest yourself, and I command you to be silent." Then, as the Holy Spirit prompted, I started calling out demons by name and telling them to flee and be gone in the name of Jesus. Most of this happened interiorly, and the outside observer would have seen me sitting next to the young man with my hand on his shoulder, praying quietly in tongues.

Interiorly, I experienced tremendous pushback. These demons didn't want to go. They knew that they had to bend the knee to the name of Jesus, but they clung to their host. I felt the presence of an evil that almost overwhelmed me, like a great invisible hand pushing against me and trying to crush me. In my mind's eye, however, I could see the demon as a little, shriveled imp. A pathetic creature terrified of losing its home.

As I continued to pray in tongues, I suddenly saw the demon fly out, and the young man exhaled deeply. For some reason, a demon's departure will often come with a physical reaction like a sigh, yawn, coughing, vomiting, or even uncontrollable screaming. I'm really glad this kid didn't start puking everywhere. I then prayed for the Holy Spirit to come in and dwell in the dark places the demon had vacated.

The young man snapped out of his reverie, but he acted drunk. I remember the ecstatic feeling from the first time I'd received deliverance from an evil spirit, so I recognized what was going on. He was experiencing the presence of the Holy Spirit. I told him to ask Jesus's forgiveness for summoning the demon. He did so. Then he said, "Jesus is AWESOME." He was so happy.

This poor kid got ensnared by the lure of evil. Human beings are created for the supernatural, for God specifically, and so we long for it. The picture of the world painted by materialists is so bleak, boring — not to mention wrong — that young people stumble into the occult without realizing that the danger is real. If you try to summon a demon, you might end up summoning a demon.

And it's not just young people either. Hollywood, of course, is completely obsessed with demons, magic, and supernatural powers. Have you noticed that most of the big movies nowadays feature grown men who wear tights and have supernatural powers? Or have you noticed the movies that make it look like witchcraft is a neutral or even good thing, depending on the attitude of the person behind the wand? Unfortunately, that is not the case.

Supernatural power comes from one of two sources. On the one hand, you have the power of the Holy Spirit dwelling in the souls of Christians. You see this power in the lives of the saints. It is always and forever linked with the name of Jesus.

Magic and witchcraft, on the other hand, are always linked with the devil and opposed to the work of God. I learned more about witchcraft while I was in prison.

I was only visiting. I volunteered to be one of the retreat leaders for Kairos Prison Ministries. It's a remarkable ministry that has been around for many years and equips guys like me to host a three-day retreat inside a prison. The structure of the retreat is a lot like the famous Cursillo or Walk to Emmaus retreats.

The goal of the retreat is to show the men in prison the love of God and teach them the plan of salvation. We want them to come to know Jesus and how much He loves them.

Kairos is ecumenical, so during the retreat, Catholic priests stand shoulder to shoulder with Methodist ministers and Lutheran pastors. Seeing different denominations working together to love them always makes a strong impression on the prisoners. Christian unity always has that effect whenever we can manage it.

The first day I went into prison for the retreat, I felt pretty scared. It's a high max prison and houses a lot of guys who have done bad, bad things. But God poured out so much grace.

Before the retreatants started to walk into the meeting room, I heard the Lord say to me, "These are my sons, I want you to love them." From that moment until the end of the retreat, three days later, I experienced no fear at all.

One of the men that I met in prison was a former Wiccan — a very passionate guy. When I told him my testimony about how the devil is real, he shared his story.

As a Wiccan, one of his religious practices was invoking the "spirits" through carefully planned rituals. While this sounds very spiritual and Earth Mother friendly, he explained that it means they summon demons and invite those demons to possess them.

This guy told me that it worked. He blacked out during the ceremony. When he came to his senses, he found that he had beaten his wife nearly to death. The incident led to ten years in prison.

He was very sorry for his sins. He loved Jesus passionately because the minister who evangelized him also cast a bunch of demons out of him. To his credit, he didn't blame the devil for beating his wife half to death or for his prison sentence. He knew he was responsible for his actions. And he knew that he needed a Savior.

I pity anyone who gets involved with witchcraft. Something about the power that might be there attracts people. Sadly, it offers so much less than what God offers to those who would repent and be baptized.

Satan ensnared Adam and Eve with the promise that they would become like God. He lied. All his promises are lies. Adam and Eve did not become like God when they ate the forbidden fruit. They became like the devil. Rebellious, ashamed, sorrowful, miserable.

God's response to this sin amazes me. Through baptism, He offers us the chance to . . . become like God. To become participants in the divine nature through the Holy Spirit dwelling in us.

These two promises — the false promise to become like God through theft and rebellion, and the true promise to become like God through His gift and our obedience — have created two kingdoms. The magic kingdom and the kingdom of God. The war between these two kingdoms has been going on for a long time.

I heard a story told by an exorcist from Washington, DC, that described a little skirmish in this war. He received a visit by a nun who was having some "troubles." She lived in Massachusetts, and some of her friends decided to take her to Salem, Massachusetts, for her birthday. They thought it would be fun and entertaining.

Salem has become a hotbed for witchcraft. The city has stores devoted to witchcraft paraphernalia, witch themed restaurants, a museum of witchcraft, and witch themed gift stores. They're trying to get as much marketing mileage out of the Salem witch trials as possible, and it's working.

The nun's two friends, who were nuns from another religious order, told her they thought that it would be fun to go into one of the witch stores and look around.

When they walked into the shop, three women in long black dresses stopped what they were doing and turned to look at them. All of them wore pentacles, the traditional symbol of witchcraft. They worked there. They didn't say a word but watched the nuns the entire time they were in the store. The nuns felt a little creeped out by this, so after a few minutes, they turned around and walked out.

"Father," the nun told the exorcist, "that night I had a sexual dream that was so horrifically violent that I woke up vomiting. And that wasn't the last of it. Night after night, I have these horrible dreams, so dark and perverted that it makes me sick. I feel like I'm going crazy."

The exorcist chastised her for doing something as stupid as going into a store run by witches. There she was, dressed in the garments of the bride of Christ, strolling into the stronghold of women who had consecrated themselves to His enemy.

He explained to her that witches (the real kind, not the cute ones made popular by British authors) make compacts with evil spirits in exchange for spiritual power. The witches in that store had summoned a demon to attack her, and that demon was the source of the violent sexual dreams.

The exorcist forgave the nun's sins through the sacrament of reconciliation and then prayed a simple exorcism prayer over her. The prayer knocked the nun off her feet. She collapsed on the ground. When she got up, she told the exorcist, "Father, it's gone." She went on to explain that ever since that day in Salem, an evil presence had afflicted her, the feeling that she was covered with an invisible, slimy . . . something. She described the sensation of being afflicted by a demon. When the demon fled the exorcism prayer, the sensation of its presence vanished.

You see, the battle is lopsided. God is infinitely powerful. Satan, though immensely powerful himself or compared to human beings, is entirely dependent on God for his existence. Any power that he has was given to him by God, and he only still has it because God does not take back a gift once given.

It only took a simple prayer from a priest trained to fight

the devil to free the nun from the demonic oppression. Even I, with my limited training and understanding, was able to deliver the young man from the evil spirit that was afflicting him. God gives this power to trample on serpents and scorpions to all who believe in His Son.

But we have to know about this power and use it. A bazooka is no help in a gunfight if it's locked in the trunk of the car.

Several years later, I ran into the young man who I prayed over when I was giving another talk. He had crazy colored hair and was wearing a pentacle like the witches in Salem. This was at a Catholic high school. He had chosen his kingdom.

# CHAPTER 9

# A love story

> *Raphael said to him: "Do you not remember your father's commands? He*
> *ordered you to marry a woman from your own ancestral family. Now listen*
> *to me, brother; do not worry about that demon. Take Sarah. I know that*
> *tonight she will be given to you as your wife! When you go into the bridal*
> *chamber, take some of the fish's liver and the heart, and place them on the*
> *embers intended for incense, and an odor will be given off. As soon as the*
> *demon smells the odor, it will flee and never again show itself near her. Then*
> *when you are about to have intercourse with her, both of you must first get*
> *up to pray. Beg the Lord of heaven that mercy and protection be granted*
> *you. Do not be afraid, for she was set apart for you before the world existed.*
> *You will save her, and she will go with you. And I assume that you will have*
> *children by her, and they will be like brothers for you. So do not worry."*
>
> (TOBIT 6:16-18)

GOD'S BEST STORIES ARE love stories. He is Love. So, of course, love is what He does best. Thankfully, mine didn't involve any fish guts on our wedding night.

For several years after my conversion, the Lord very explicitly told me to remain single for a season. A long season. About three years. I whined a lot to pretty much everyone, but it didn't offend Him. He kept in mind my prayer to receive the best He had to offer. It just took that much time for Him to file off the rust and polish me up in preparation for the one He had chosen.

While I complained about being single down in Georgia, Mary Germann lived in the Bronx under the name Sister Mary Angelica, a second-year novice with the Sisters of Life. She felt the call to religious life in high school, so after getting her bachelor's degree in philosophy at Christendom College, she went off to the convent. In 2010, she was preparing to take vows with the order, but the Lord said to her in prayer, "Trust me in what I'm about to do."

Seemingly out of nowhere, the desire to be married, to have a more concrete relationship, began to well up in her heart. On the feast of Divine Mercy Sunday, Sister Mary Angelica went out to pray next to a statue of Our Lady of Fatima — her personal favorite. The question of marriage burned in her heart, and she cried out to the Blessed Mother, asking if there was a man out there whom she could love and share her life. In the quiet of her heart, she heard the response, "His name is Nathan." She responded, "Nathan? I don't know any Nathans!" and decided to ignore it completely.

Still, the desire to be married grew and grew until she finally went to her novice director and essentially said, "I don't think I'm supposed to be a sister," to which her novice director replied, "Yes, dear, we know." Four days later, she boarded a plane to her parent's house in Georgia.

This experience traumatized her somewhat, like breaking off an engagement, but she knew that the Lord had a plan.

Shortly after arriving home, she went with her sister to the Adoration Chapel to pray on the Feast of Our Lady of Fatima. Her prayer stopped when I came in, threw myself down in front of the altar, and began to weep. Brian died that day. My sorrow moved her profoundly. She also somehow knew that she would marry me. On the way home, she learned from her sister that my name was Nathan.

We did not officially meet until several weeks later, on the Feast of Pentecost. I stood behind Mike's house in Center Circle, cracking a bullwhip I made of parachute cord. Mary and her sister Amy, a good friend of mine, came up to say hello. Amy introduced me as Nathan, and we shook hands. Mary felt as if lightning struck her, and she thought, "This is him! THIS IS MY HUSBAND!" She did not, however, say this aloud, but rather something more along the lines of, "Hi. Nice to meet you." I was completely oblivious. We chatted for a moment, and then I went back to cracking the whip.

Mary percolated on this for a few days before going to her mother and saying, "Mom, I think I'm going to marry Nathan Krupa." Her mother responded, "Oh, that's nice, dear. I like him. If it's from the Lord, it'll happen. You'll just have to wait and see." Mary agreed with her mom and decided to wait to see what the Lord had in store for her. Mary can be very patient and has a will of finely-honed steel from her time with the Sisters. It would take longer than she expected.

I ignored her completely. For three years, I begged God to show me the woman He wanted me to marry. I mean this very literally because I realized that I was too foolish to decide something that important. I wanted God to lead me to the woman He wanted me to marry, and I only ever wanted to date that one woman. In the Book of Tobit, the angel Raphael tells the young man Tobias that the woman he wanted to marry had been set apart for him before the foundation of the world. That was the kind of woman that I wanted to marry — the one that God had created specifically to marry ME. The best He had to offer. He said yes to this prayer but told me that I had to do it His way or I would never even meet her.

Doing things His way meant waiting . . . and waiting . . . and waiting. I prayed over and over for the best He had to offer. I asked Him to close the door to anyone who was not 'THE ONE.' He did. Time and again. My fingers got bloody clinging to the door jamb every time He closed a door. I would get what I thought were signs from God that I should marry some woman, only to watch with horror as she got engaged and married someone else. When Mary showed up, I had convinced myself that God wanted me to marry someone else and completely ignored the sound of the door slamming and the pain in my hands. So, God sent me a prophet. I also ignored him . . . for a while.

One day, my friend, Big Dan, called me up. I call him Big Dan because he's ex-military, about 6' 6," and looks like he could arm wrestle a polar bear. He's awesome, and for a season, God spoke to him powerfully through visions. He said, "Hey dude, I just had a vision . . . of your wedding." "What? !? !?" I replied. "Yeah, I saw the whole thing." "Did you see who I was going to marry?" "Yup." I freaked out for a moment interiorly before saying, "Stop. Don't say a word. I don't want to hear it. If it is from the Lord, it will happen without you telling me. If it's from the devil, I will do something stupid and ruin everything." I paused for a moment before asking, "Is she cute?" "Oh, she's beautiful!" "Ok, stop right there. Don't tell me anything else." I hung up, and that was that.

A couple of months later, he called me up again. "Nathan, you're an idiot. It is Mary Germann. That's who I saw in the vision of your wedding." I started to get angry at him, but I stopped short. Mary Germann. HMM. Former nun, so she's holy. Valedictorian of her class, so she's brilliant. Beautiful. Raised in Alleluia, charismatic, Catholic. I had noticed her in daily mass more than a few times, which indicated that she was serious about practicing her faith. My curiosity flared up. I yelled at Dan for telling me against my wishes, but I only half meant it.

Still, at that point, I wanted to date someone else ... and pry open a door that God wanted closed, which meant I was getting crushed in the process. He is the God who can close doors that NO ONE can open, so He was winning. I told Big Dan to pray that God's will be done while I waited for God to let me date the lady I'd set my sights on. If God wanted me to marry Mary Germann, He would have to make it happen.

It took a couple more months of stubborn suffering on my part before I realized that the person behind door number one was reserved for another contestant. The suffering was very healing and redemptive because it forced me to look at the giant, burnt-out tree stump in my heart from the relationship that crashed and burned in Los Angeles. God pulled out the heavy earth moving equipment to uproot that nasty old stump and prepare the soil for something new. He had to prepare me for Mary.

Mary and I found ourselves in a fairly unique situation. Both of us had received what we thought were prophecies from the Lord that we were going to marry the other. Neither of us wanted to start the conversation, "So . . . I think God wants us to get married" for fear of the other fleeing in terror. So instead of jumping in with both feet, we just dipped our toes in the water to test the temperature. Mary was, and is, a firm believer that it is not ladylike for a young woman to pursue a man. She did, however, agree with Emily Post that a little bit of cat-like stalking is appropriate. Little did I know, but her appearances at daily mass, sitting directly across from me, were anything but accidental. We would 'accidentally' bump into each other on the way out and exchange polite nothings as we walked out of the church. All part of Mary's devious plan.

One day, our conversation wandered into some theological question. Mary had a thought after mass about a topic that she wanted to share with me. She got my phone number from her sister and sent her thoughts to me by text message. This was divinely inspired courage. When I got the message, I was pleasantly surprised. I love chewing on theology and trying to understand my place in God's universe, so I sent a thoughtful response back. This little seed began to grow into one of those thoroughly modern romances known as the text message flirtation. She would send me a loooooong message about some passage from the Psalms. I would respond with a looooong message about something that St. Francis said that spoke about the same passage. It was all very spiritual and very pure. And super nerdy. I was impressed by her thoughtfulness and enjoyed getting to know her.

It was maybe October when I got 'The Letter.' "Dear Nathan, we've heard that you might be interested in the Priesthood. Come to our Diocesan Vocations retreat and find out what

God wants you to do with your life." WHAT! ? Just because I'm over 30 and single? I didn't want to be a priest. I wanted to be married. I took the letter to Mike, whose son happens to be a priest and the chancellor of the Diocese — I still don't think getting the letter was a coincidence — and told him about it. When I said that I didn't want to go, he asked if I was dating anyone. He knew the answer was no, but I said so anyway. He asked me why I was going to turn down a free retreat. I said, "Right. I'll go."

This was terrible. What if God said I was supposed to be a priest? What if He intended to stretch the three years of not dating into a lifetime of celibacy? ACK! I signed up to go, even as I began praying fervently that I didn't want to be a priest, but I would if He wanted me to be. The retreat was in December, so I spent the next two months dreading His answer. I told Mary all about it, but I don't think that she worried quite as much as I did. Finally, the day arrived for me to drive down to Macon, GA to seek God's will.

About 40 miles outside of Augusta, the transmission on my little green Honda started to have a nervous breakdown. Suddenly, my smooth trip began to have the herky-jerky feel of a rollercoaster as it climbs to the top of the first big drop. I stopped and called my friend Andy so that we could pray over the car. The car started moving after we finished, so I decided to continue to my destination. About 20 miles outside of Macon, the transmission started flipping out again. I was going 15 mph, then 50, then 20, back and forth, as it would catch just enough to get over the next hill before flipping out again. At this point, I was praying, "Lord, I didn't even want to go to this in the first place, but PLEASE GET ME TO THIS RETREAT."

Finally, after about an hour and a half, my car sputtered into the parking lot of the Church of the Holy Spirit in Macon. I was so happy to get there that I completely forgot that I didn't want to be there.

The retreat was awesome. It featured talks by several priests and seminarians, some informative videos, and time spent praying silently in the sanctuary. God spoke to me very clearly. He did not want me to be a priest. He wanted me to go back to Alleluia, get married, and have a family. I was thrilled, delighted, relieved. I told the priest in charge that I wanted to leave my car in the parking lot and figure out what to do about it later. I caught a ride home to Augusta with a friend who also went on the retreat.

By the end of the next day, I bought a red Chevy truck from another member of the community and donated the green Honda to the church in Macon. I didn't have a vehicle for only one day. I talked with my spiritual director about the retreat and told him what God had said. I also told him about my text messaging Mary and Big Dan's vision. He said that he would pray about it and get back to me.

Three days before Christmas, Mike and I sat down over a cold glass of Chimay Ale. He said, "You know what you asked me about Mary Germann . . . I feel pretty peaceful about you asking her out. I think that may be what the Lord is doing in your life." I was ecstatic. I had the green light to ask a woman out for the first time in three years. I started thinking about how I would do it. I obsessed over it because I hadn't asked anyone out in years. Then, on Christmas Day, the Holy Spirit said, "Ask her out." I said, "When?" He said, "NOW!" In the heat of the moment, I sent her a text message inviting her out to coffee. The waiting was terrible. It took more than an hour before my phone buzzed. "Sure. That sounds fun." Best. Christmas. Present. EVER!

Our first date was very nearly a disaster. I planned to take Mary out for coffee — something low key. After I picked her up, we drove to the coffee shop I had picked out only to discover that it was closed for the night. I was a little mortified, but I told her that my plan was not God's plan. I prayed aloud for God to guide the date and then drove another 10 minutes to a Starbucks. It was packed, so we ended up sitting outside on a brisk winter night. We both wore heavy wool coats, but the chill seeped through.

I decided that I needed to tell her all about my nervous breakdown, dramatic conversion, and battles with the devil. This was a make or break moment. I recognized the distinct possibility that she might run screaming into the night and never look back. I wanted to tell her sooner rather than later so that I wouldn't get my heart broken six months down the line when she realized I was a bit . . . different. She took it calmly, and when I asked her if she would prefer to walk around to get our blood flowing, she agreed. I decided that the parking lot of a strip mall was not a great place for a romantic stroll, so we hopped back into the car and drove to the Riverwalk downtown. As we strolled along the river, we continued talking about adventures in the spiritual life. She took my confession quite well at the time, though I found out later that she asked her sister Amy if I was crazy. Amy told her, "No, that's just Nathan."

Ultimately, the date went well enough that I asked her to go out again, and she agreed. During the next date, we discussed Alleluia. Her parents are members of the community, as are her two older brothers and their families, but she had not taken that step yet herself. The date itself went better, as I had done a little more advanced planning and found a wine tasting at a local shop. We learned that we both like a nice glass of wine, and she did a little more of the talking this time. I have to be careful because she is an introvert and I am an extrovert. If I don't stop and try to listen, she never gets a word in edgewise.

At the end of the date, I invited Mary to go out again. Mary told me that she had discussed our relationship with one of the older ladies in the community, who recommended that we should only see each other in larger groups for a while. Mary thought this was a good idea so that we didn't get too far too fast. I don't know how well I managed to contain my internal freak-out, but I said, "Well, if that is what you need, praise God. We can do that. God has a plan."

I think this would have started a total self-destruct sequence on my part, except that God did have a plan. In the next week, I received two random invitations from friends for group activities. Mary showed up to both, and I took the opportunity to chat with her. It was very good because I got to see her in a more social setting. I pushed the envelope a little bit and set up a game night with a married couple who are close friends. Everything seemed to be moving swiftly along.

Then came Valentine's Day. It's a day that strikes terror into the hearts of young lovers everywhere. Will she be my Valentine? Won't she? It's cute when you're seven, and you can pass out Valentine's cards to every girl in your 2nd-grade class with the expectation that at least one will check the box marked "Yes." When one is 33 and still single, the experience can feel more like jumping into the shark tank wearing armor made of tuna steaks.

As a culture, our expectations for Valentine's Day have gotten a little ridiculous. We have spent too much time watching
romantic comedies where the hero takes his girl on a private
jet to Paris for dinner before proposing to her at the top of the
Eiffel Tower using a marching band at the base that spells out
"Will You Marry Me?" while playing "All You Need is Love" by
the Beatles (I don't know if this exact scenario has ever been
in a movie, but I would not be surprised).

Since I do not own a private jet, I had to scale my plans
down. I gave her a single red rose at the beginning of the date
when I picked her up that night. I took her out to a nice restaurant with live bluegrass music. The music was quiet enough to
talk, the wine was tasty, and the food was delicious. Afterward,
we decided to stroll out beside the river. It was not terribly cold,
but we were both bundled up in our black woolen overcoats.

We sat down on a bench that overlooked the river and
chatted for a while. A lull came in the conversation. This was
THE MOMENT! I could almost hear the angels singing in the
background. I gathered my courage before ardently saying, "I
would like to kiss you right now. May I?" She paused a moment
before responding, "You may kiss me on the forehead, but not
on the lips." Imagine my surprise. I started laughing.

We took a moment to gather our wits. I told her that the old
Nathan would allow one or two dates maximum to get the first
kiss before calling the whole thing off. No patience whatsoever.
But God had changed me, and I confessed that I was in love
with her whether she kissed me or not. She responded to me
that she was in love with me, as well. Delight filled us both.
The confession of mutual love was, in fact, better than any kiss
I had ever received. We floated about two feet off the ground

on our way back to my truck. We marveled that the Lord had given us a chaste love for one another and that it was better than any physical expression of love we had ever experienced.

Romantic comedies have certainly programmed our thinking that the first kiss is the ultimate expression of love. They have also taught us to think that Valentine's Day without a first kiss is an abominable failure that can only be rectified by going to ridiculous lengths to secure the first kiss. The movies have more subtly taught that a virtuous woman who resists the advances of men is destined to be an old maid people call "the cat lady." Hollywood teaches us that we need the freedom to love without all the outdated "rules" about physical intimacy.

I discovered on that particular Valentine's Day that romantic comedies don't know anything about love. Love can be expressed in a most delightful way without any physical intimacy whatsoever. A failed attempt at a first kiss can be a brilliant success and source of great joy. A virtuous woman who can gently and lovingly resist the advances of the man she loves can be the most desirable of women. Most importantly, a love that is authored by the King of Love is pure, and purity is freedom.

Valentine's Day ended with an effervescent declaration of mutual love instead of a kiss. Subsequent discussions revealed that we both felt like God was calling us to marry one another. But we didn't feel like it was quite the time yet. One of my favorite verses from the Song of Songs is, "Do not awaken love before its time" (SONG 8:4). This verse applied to our situation. Imagine trying to force a rosebud into full bloom before it is ready. You will destroy it.

I told her about God instilling the Fear of God in me, and that I would begin asking Him if it was ok to give her a goodnight kiss after our dates. She very patiently accepted this. If it drove her crazy, she never mentioned it. For the first month, He always told me, "No." The next month? "No." The month after that? "No." I have more sympathy for Adam and Eve now. The allure of forbidden fruit only increases with time. It got to the point where I would just say, "I have to go now," get up, and leave. She knew what I meant and said, "Goodbye."

One nice thing about this restriction on physical intimacy is that we spent hours and hours talking to one another. We spent almost as many hours praying together. At the price of physical intimacy, we reaped a return of emotional, spiritual, and mental intimacy. Mary had enough time to discern that the Lord also wanted her to join Alleluia, so we agreed that it was where God wanted us. More months passed, and still the Lord told me, "No." He did allow me to hold her hand and eventually give her a hug, but never the first kiss. One of the things that our culture has forgotten with the advent of immediate gratification relationships is that holding hands can be awesome. A hug can be thrilling. If you skip these things in your race to the bedroom, you are robbing yourself of a sweet, pure, and irreplaceable treat.

At some point during this process, the Lord gave me a vision of two people being drawn together like the halves of a zipper. If you try to rush a zipper, all you do is break it. The zipper started with the spiritual before we even met when we were praying for each other without knowing it. The zipper then joined us mentally and emotionally as we came to know and love one another. Last of all was the physical. We were grateful for this vision because we could see the point of what God was doing.

I went on a pilgrimage that August to Spain and World

Youth Day. It was an incredible trip on every level and something that I will never forget. When I got back, I felt like the Lord was about to do something, but I didn't know what. I took Mary to daily Mass, which we had been doing every day for several months. Both of us felt kind of frustrated with waiting.

Sitting in a pew after Mass, I asked the Lord what He was doing. He gave me a vision that made me laugh. I told Mary, "The Lord just gave me a vision of a quiche. The sense of what He means by this is that if you are making quiche and you're supposed to cook it for an hour at 300 degrees, you can't cook it for half an hour at 600 degrees and still expect to get quiche. It will be done when it's done." It wasn't very comforting, frankly. As we left the church, I blurted out, "You know what would be awesome? A brie quiche!" I happen to love brie cheese. "What else would you put on it?" Mary asked. "Bacon . . . and mushrooms." I walked her out to her car, gave her a long goodbye hug, and went off to work.

That night at dinner, my spiritual director Mike made an offhanded comment, "We need to talk about timing." My ears perked up. I found out later that Mary had talked to his wife Bev about not wanting to wait any longer. After dinner, I grabbed Mike and asked, "What did you mean by timing?" We both knew what he was talking about. "Well, what are you waiting for?" "I am waiting on the Lord to tell me to move. I don't know when that will be." "Do you have any doubts that you're supposed to marry her?" "No." "Does she have any doubts that she is supposed to marry you?" "No." "So, what are you waiting for?" It dawned on me that Mike was again giving me the green light. "Do you think it's time?" I asked. "Do you see any reason why not?" A wave of elation swept over me. "Yes.

Yes, it is time!" I gave him a big hug. We discussed it a little further, and I decided that I needed to ask her father's permission
before I asked her to marry me. As God would have it, we had
already planned to go to her parents for dinner that Sunday
for a barbecue because it was Labor Day weekend.

So on Sunday afternoon, we went out to the country
where Mary grew up. My mind was filled with the prospect
of asking Mary's dad for her hand in marriage. I wasn't so
much scared as I just didn't know what to expect. When I
had asked Jerry many months previously for permission to
court Mary, he prayed about it for a week or so before saying
yes. I expected him to tell me that he would pray about it
and get back to me. More waiting, but I felt like I was in
the final stretch.

I found a moment out by the BBQ pit when I could talk to
him alone. "Jerry, I think that the Lord wants Mary and me
to get married, and I would like to have your permission." A
moment's pause. "Well, praise the Lord. That's wonderful. Let
me pray for you." He prayed a beautiful and sincere prayer for
us and the coming engagement. When he finished, he talked
to me about how to honor Mary as a wife and to treat her the
way I should. As I listened, my heart was sailing! Another
green light. I could hardly contain myself on the drive home.

I talked to Mike that night and told him that Jerry had
approved the match. When I mentioned that I needed to get
an engagement ring, he responded, "You don't need an engagement ring if you're in love. I didn't buy Bev a ring until after
she said that she would marry me. Isn't that right, dear?" Bev
affirmed that a ring isn't really necessary. My heart was explod-
ing. Suddenly, all the barriers to proposing marriage had been

swept away. I was filled with peace, but more excited than I have ever been in my entire life. The next day was Labor Day. I would do it then.

I picked Mary up the next morning to take her to daily Mass. I could hardly contain myself, but somehow, I managed not to say anything. After Mass, we sat in the quiet church, and it very nearly exploded out of me. Unfortunately, some random people wandered around the sanctuary, so it didn't quite feel exactly right. I decided to take Mary home because we planned to eat breakfast together.

When we walked into her home, I noticed that a beautiful Ave Maria was playing in the background and something smelled wonderful. Mary smiled bashfully as she pointed to the stove. Cooling on the stovetop was a quiche. Made with brie. And bacon. And mushrooms. The quiche was done, and it was delicious. After we each ate a slice, a stillness filled the air.

"I talked to your dad yesterday, and he gave me permission to ask you for your hand in marriage. Will you marry me?"

"You're asking me to marry you, RIGHT NOW! ?"

I came around the table and fell to my knees. "Will you marry me?" She fell to her knees. "YES!" I sealed our love with our very . . . first . . . kiss.

My years of waiting for my wife came to an end four months later, the shortest possible time allowed by the Church. Our relationship survived the engagement, which is a marvel considering the stress of planning a wedding and preparing to start a life together. The wedding itself was a flurry of activity.

The memory that blazes like a lighthouse is seeing her walk down the aisle toward me in her beautiful wedding gown. I never knew such joy was possible.

# CHAPTER 10

# Take up your cross

*My child, when you come to serve the Lord, prepare yourself for trials. Be sincere of heart and steadfast, and do not be impetuous in time of adversity. Cling to him, do not leave him, that you may prosper in your last days. Accept whatever happens to you; in periods of humiliation be patient. For in fire gold is tested, and the chosen, in the crucible of humiliation. Trust in God, and he will help you; make your ways straight and hope in him. You that fear the Lord, wait for his mercy, do not stray lest you fall. You that fear the Lord, trust in him, and your reward will not be lost. You that fear the Lord, hope for good things, for lasting joy and mercy. Consider the generations long past and see: has anyone trusted in the Lord and been disappointed? Has anyone persevered in his fear and been forsaken? Has anyone called upon him and been ignored? For the Lord is compassionate and merciful; forgives sins and saves in time of trouble.*

(SIRACH 2:1-11)

GOD HAD DONE BIG things in my life. He had given me a beautiful, holy wife. He'd given me a huge crowd of new friends and a community to share my life. He had called me to serve the poor. Although I had never done any grant writing, I discovered that I have a bit of a knack for it. In fact, in the time that I've been at the food bank, I've raised millions of dollars to feed the hungry. I was at a point where I was good at my job. My co-workers respected me. I raised lots of money. I loved to write. I loved what I was doing. It filled me with great joy.

Everything is awesome, right? It'll be smooth sailing from here until eternity, right?

Wrong!

One day, the Lord asked me if I would prefer to suffer at work or at home. Since I was newly and happily married, the choice seemed easy and obvious. I told Him that if I had to choose one or the other, I would prefer to suffer at work.

When you come to serve the Lord, prepare yourselves for trials. Take up your cross daily and all that. I didn't realize that God meant "suffering." Like real suffering that gets down into your bones.

The devil discovered that he was having difficulty seducing me into sin by exciting a desire for sin, so he changed tactics.

The early monks wrote about a demon called "Acedia." Remember that demons are often called by type of sin or spiritual attack they inspire. Acedia is a type of desolation that makes doing good feel bad. Instead of the joy that should come from good works, the demon Acedia gives us sorrow, darkness and internal turmoil.

Legions of these nasty critters came after me.

Out of nowhere, a dark time started. Overnight, I went from loving my job to despising it. I couldn't explain it. Nothing had changed on the outside. I was still good at what I did, still successful, still respected, but suddenly going to work every day was a major battle. No joy in writing, which I love to do. No joy when a check came in from a grant. Not a drop of satisfaction or feeling of accomplishment when checks came in that were bigger than my annual salary.

I would sit at my desk staring at my computer, thinking about the deadlines that were coming up, unable to put my hands on the keyboard until the very last minute. I needed every ounce of effort and will power to type a paragraph. Putting words on paper felt like filing my soul with a rasp. If you don't know what a rasp is, Google it. They take out big chunks.

It got worse. Every day, thoughts of quitting my job battered me. Every meeting with my boss was consumed by a desire to rage, shout, and storm out of the office, never to return. Dread filled my soul every weekday morning when I woke up because I had another day of work ahead of me.

You might be asking yourself why I didn't go on anti-depressants and call it a day. This is an important question. Mental illness and depression are real things. Sometimes the chemistry in our brains stops working the way it should. Scientists have found ways to alter our brain chemistry to give us some relief from unnecessary suffering.

Something clued me in to the fact that this was not mental illness. The moment I walked out the door at 5:00 or went home for the weekend, the darkness lifted. With the suddenness of opening a window in a smoky room and breathing fresh air, I felt better. I experienced the kind of relief that you have when you stretch open your hand after you've held something heavy for too long.

I discussed what was going on with Mike, my spiritual director. He affirmed that I was experiencing the cross. Jesus told us, "Whoever wishes to come after me must deny himself, take up his cross, and follow me. For whoever wishes to save his life will lose it, but whoever loses his life for my sake will find it." (MATTHEW 16:24-25) I was shocked to discover that He actually meant it and that by "cross" He meant real honest-to-goodness suffering.

Jesus grew up under the authority of Rome. He knew that crucifixion caused horrific suffering. He probably saw crucifixions growing up. The Romans made a public spectacle of crucifixion to quell crime and rebellion. It was cruel and unusual on purpose. Jesus's disciples knew all of this, too.

When Jesus told His disciples to take up their crosses, they must have scratched their heads and looked at Him with head-tilted incomprehension. Only years later, when all but one of His apostles died horrific deaths did it make sense. To oppose the devil is to embrace suffering for the love of God and the love of our fellow man.

Take up your cross and follow Him. It's not a sanitized, decorated piece of popular jewelry, but a heavy, brutal, wicked instrument of torture. Christ Himself dropped His cross because it was too heavy, and He was so weak from being scourged.

The reality of this level of suffering, the invitation to suffer, should make us stop and pause. But it's important to know that this is not the whole story.

During this season of darkness and toil, the Lord gave me a gift of determination and fortitude that didn't make sense to me. For months I prayed every morning, "Lord, help me to set my face like flint." I knew that I was supposed to be at the food bank, I knew I was supposed to be raising money, and I knew that God would give me the grace that I needed to stay as long as He wanted me to.

St. Ignatius of Loyola came to the rescue with his 14 rules for discernment of spirits.[1] In a nutshell, St. Ignatius teaches that everything awesome that we experience comes from God, and everything that sucks comes from the devil. It makes sense if you think about it. God, being all good and loving, would want us to experience good things. The devil, being completely evil and separated from everything good, doesn't have anything to offer EXCEPT things that suck and are terrible.

The rules also provide clear guidance for what to do when experiencing the devil's attacks, which St. Ignatius calls desolation. If the desolation comes from the decision to sin, then the solution is to turn from sin and repent. If the desolation comes from the decision to do some good thing that you've prayerfully chosen, keep going. When you're walking through a dark, rat-infested tunnel, keep walking. It won't last forever.

Rule number eight says something like, "When in a period of desolation, keep in mind that it won't last forever." I clung to this rule like a life raft. One September day, when I thought that I couldn't take it anymore, I said to myself, "I can keep going until Christmas."

Christmas came and went. "I can keep going until my birthday." April came and went; I kept going. "I can keep going

---

1  Fr. Timothy Gallagher has written an exceptional book on the 14 rules of discernment called *Discernment of Spirits*. He has a real gift for teaching the material and also hosts free podcasts on the subject that are excellent at www.discerninghearts.com.

until . . ." I lived the next two years going month to month. Sometimes I had to tell myself: "I can make it to Friday."

Over the next couple of years, the intense desolation slowly decreased. Until one day, I noticed that getting up and going to work was no longer a battle. My work no longer caused me to pull at the swiftly retreating remnants of my hair but started to become fun again. I (re)discovered my love for raising money, so much so that I started a website and wrote a book focused on fundraising for the Church and ministry.[2]

This experience taught me a lot. First of all, God wanted to make a point about the cross. Suffering is not optional. It's mandatory. "Son though He was, He learned obedience through what He suffered." (HEBREWS 5:8) If you want to learn obedience to God, prepare for trials.

But also keep in mind that the cross is not the end of the story. The Romans crucified countless people. I worship only One — the One who didn't stay dead. The Resurrection takes the cross and transforms it from an instrument of brutal cruelty and oppression into a sign of divine hope for the ages.

Going through a period of intense suffering gave me an opportunity to experience the power of the Resurrection. God was at work doing something inside me.

The Bible gives a great image of how God purifies us "like gold refined in a fire." How does a goldsmith purify gold? He puts gold in a crucible and heats it until it melts. Then he pours in a substance called flux, which brings all of the impurities to the surface. The impurities float on the gold because the gold is denser. The goldsmith scrapes the junk (called dross) off the

---

2   thealmoner.com and Letters from the Almoner. (Shameless plug)

top and throws it away. Then he repeats this process until no dross remains, and he can see his reflection on the surface of the molten metal.

Gold doesn't feel the melting or the flux or the ladle scraping out the junk. The human soul does. When God purifies us, He turns up the heat. He throws in some change (flux is another word for change) to bring all our flaws to the surface. Then He scrapes the junk away, leaving a purified soul behind. If that doesn't sound painful, give it some more thought.

And yet, this parable gives us a beautiful understanding of how God sees us. He sees the gold in us because He put it there. He also sees the junk, the impurities, and He chooses to do something about it. Since He created us, He knows exactly how to remove our flaws, and He loves us so much that He's unwilling to allow all that garbage to remain. He loves us enough to enable us to endure suffering that cleanses us.

When our purification comes to completion, then we can reflect His light to the world. If He allowed the impurities to remain, His image in us would be perpetually distorted.

When Jesus tells us to take up our cross daily, He's not talking about a piece of jewelry. He's talking about suffering that purifies and makes us beautiful, suffering that reaches down into the darkest corners of our souls. But that suffering bears good fruit; it removes our sins and fears and fruitless desires. He wants us to take up the cross so that we can pass through it to the mystery of the Resurrection and be free to love.

During this purification, the Lord showed me a lot about the good that I failed to do. Sins of omission.

One day, I went to lunch with a group of 6 or 7 people. As we walked out after eating — some of us with to-go boxes in hand — an older man approached us, looking for something to eat. The leader of our group expressed some irritation and shooed him away from us. We all walked back to our cars.

When I got back to the food bank, I sat in my car for a few minutes. "I'm a food banker, and I just walked right past that guy." I got so angry with myself. My hypocrisy was displayed for everyone to see. Here God had given me an opportunity to feed the hungry up close, and I'd walked away like everybody else.

This memory burned me for months. One moment of hardness of heart on my part, and that guy went hungry. "You saw me hungry and didn't feed me, get out of my presence, you evildoer!" (MATTHEW 25:42)

I realized that it's a lot harder to identify sins of omission (the good we should do) than sins of commission (the evil we shouldn't). The devil's attack against doing good is so cunning. He makes it distasteful, inconvenient, costly. I easily excused my sin by saying that I don't want to enable someone's bad behavior by giving them money.

My heart had to change. I asked God for a new way to think about it. I talked to my wife and spiritual director. After a bunch of prayer and consideration, I decided to do things a little differently.

I realized that $5 doesn't make a huge difference to me, sad to say, and it won't make a dent in the life of someone on the street. Five dollars won't even last through the night. But a prayer might make all the difference in the world.

So, I began to think of the money that they asked for as the price I had to pay to be able to pray with them. I have never been turned down when I asked, "May I say a prayer for you?" after handing them a fiver.

I still exercise prudence. I once gently turned down a request for a ride from a woman who was obviously high on drugs, although I did buy her a cheeseburger and pray with her.

Sometimes this is a hard thing for me to do. I'm not St. Francis with his miraculous change of heart when he chose to embrace the leper. I still struggle with being selfish, distracted, or so focused on my desires that I don't make the extra effort to serve the people around me that need my service. Sometimes my job for the food bank can even be a barrier because I justify my callousness with, "I gave at the office."

But I found that whenever I made some sacrifice to serve someone in need, God always gave me vastly more in return.

One night, I went to a big dinner hosted by one of our local United Ways branches. My wife stayed home because we had a new baby. I showed up to the venue early, because it was in a cool part of town with some neat shops.

As I walked past the event venue, an older homeless guy sitting next to the building called me over. He asked me for money. I had some time, so I said, "Why don't I buy you dinner?" He readily agreed and stood to walk with me to a restaurant.

The first restaurant we came to knew the man. "You know you aren't supposed to come in here! Get lost! Looks like you found another sucker." The waitress's anger surprised me.

The man looked at me bashfully, "There's only a couple of places that will let me come in."

"Which one is your favorite?" As we walked to a sandwich shop that he liked, he told me all about his life. I listened and asked questions. He played drums in bands as a young man, and still cherished the hopes of getting back into the music scene once he got back on his feet.

We got to the shop, ordered, and I prayed for him while we were waiting for his food. I noticed some of the other patrons of the restaurant looking with disgust at the man while I prayed. I said goodbye and went back to my gala dinner. I made it just in time.

As the awards dinner droned on and on (awards dinners are just about always boring, aren't they?), joy filled me. I bought Jesus a sandwich — from His favorite restaurant. How awesome was that?

I know that I didn't fix all of his problems, but he didn't ask me to. He asked me for a sandwich. I could do that much. And maybe my prayers ended up making a difference.

God puts the people that He wants us to love right in front of us. Remember the parable of the rich man and Lazarus (LUKE 16:19-31). Lazarus sat right at the rich man's doorstep. God made it easy for the rich man to find the person he was supposed to love.

From the sound of it, Lazarus was in pretty bad shape, with open sores all over his body that the dogs licked. But all the rich man had to do to ensure his place in Abraham's bosom was overcome his distaste and share the scraps from his table. It was a small sacrifice with long-term consequences.

The cross is the ultimate symbol of love: God's love for us and our love for the wretched on our doorstep. It's love that costs us something, that is paid for with suffering, but that leads to the Resurrection and eternal life.

And that's why Jesus tells us to take up our cross daily. It's the best advice He can give us.

# CHAPTER 11

# Fatherhood

*Then [Jesus] questioned [the boy's] father, "How long has this been happening to him?" He replied, "Since childhood. It has often thrown him into fire and into water to kill him. But if you can do anything, have compassion on us and help us." Jesus said to him, "'If you can!' Everything is possible to one who has faith." Then the boy's father cried out, "I do believe, help my unbelief!" Jesus, on seeing a crowd gathering, rebuked the unclean spirit and said to it, "Mute and deaf spirit, I command you: come out of him and never enter him again!" Shouting and throwing the boy into convulsions, it came out. He became like a corpse, which caused many to say, "He is dead!" But Jesus took him by the hand, raised him, and he stood up.*

(MARK 9:21-28)

THE DEVIL DOESN'T ALWAYS come after you directly. I discovered this when my wife and I started having children. The evil one likes to go after the weakest in the bunch. Remember, "Your opponent, the devil, is prowling around like a roaring lion looking for [someone] to devour" (1 PETER 5:8). Lions don't go after the biggest and strongest wildebeest in the herd. No, they look for the sickly ones. The ones that fall behind the others. The new calves left unattended.

Very early on, my oldest son developed trouble sleeping. Big trouble. Six or seven times a night, he would wake up screaming and crying. And I'm not talking about just normal baby crying in the middle of the night because he wants Mommy. I'm talking about the sound of a child expressing terror from the depth of his soul. I would get up to rock him back to sleep, which would take 15-20 minutes. I was so tired during that year that I thought I was going to die.

One night, when he was about a year and a half old, he had a really bad one. He started screaming and wouldn't stop. The first time I went into his room I was tired and grumpy, so I very sternly told him to stop. No points for compassion. Great job, dad. He choked back his cries, and I got him to lay back down again. Maybe half an hour later, he started screaming again. This time, Mary went in and tried to comfort him. We gave him some Tylenol in case he had a sore throat, and then some milk, but he wouldn't settle down.

I started asking him questions about what was wrong, trying to find out how I could help him. When I asked him if he had a bad dream, he stuttered, "Yes." "Was there a monster?" "MONSTER!" I laid down with him and started to pray over him. After a few minutes of prayer, he balled in his arms and hands tightly and started hissing at me. That's called a demonic manifestation. I didn't expect THAT!

I kept praying, and suddenly he deeply exhaled and relaxed. I recognized the departure of an evil spirit. He calmed down a great deal. I kept praying, and another demon fled. He was all the way calm. I asked him if he felt better. I could tell by his calm response that he was sincere. Fear itself had vanished. I explained to him that if another monster tries to scare him, to get Daddy, and I will beat that monster up and send him away. Monsters are afraid of Jesus. He went right to sleep and slept all through the night.

Mary took our son to Mass the next day, and he said, "Tank yu Djeus, monster" after she prompted him to thank Jesus for scaring away the monster. When I got home from work, he was still telling the story. "I had a bad dream. Monster chasing me. Daddy come beat up monster. Monster sad. Monster scream AAAHHH. Monster run away!" He repeated it over and over again.

I was so ashamed of the harshness of my initial reaction afterward, but I had a realization . . . my anger was stirred, not simply by my son's behavior, but also by the presence of a demon. I had an instinct of its presence, even though I didn't know it consciously. Anger and fear are the soul's two primal responses to the presence of evil. I experienced anger, and my son experienced fear. It is humiliating that, in my ignorance, my anger hurt my son rather than the demon that was attacking him.

The odds that a demon has come after you are pretty much 100 percent. I gave a talk to a bunch of high school students once, and one of the teenage boys said, "I've never been attacked by a demon." I laughed. This poor kid had the Hollywood vision of demon in his mind. A nasty imp with horns and a forked tail. Or a raging dog with glowing red eyes that flees only when doused by holy water. While there are certainly stories from the lives of the saints that describe this kind of manifestation, this is not the way that most people will experience it.

Have you ever walked into a home where things didn't feel right? Nothing that you can explain, nothing necessarily out of place, but you feel something evil? It's not necessarily the case, but often that sense of something evil can be explained by the actual presence of something evil.

One morning before dawn, I jumped rope in front of my house. Suddenly, from my left side came the feeling that something horrifically evil approached. The hair on my arms and neck shot out. Terror filled me, and it took all of my will power to keep jumping rope. I had learned my lesson and began to pray against the spirit of fear that was trying to send me fleeing into my house. After two minutes of prayer, the demon fled, and my soul filled with the peace of a cool country morning.

The fact that you're aware of spiritual presences is entirely logical. You are a body/soul composite, and the spiritual part of you is operating on the same plane of reality as the demons.

It's also entirely logical that scientific instruments fail to pick up signs of demonic activity (unless it's super obvious like objects floating through the air). Scientific instruments operate on the material level, so they won't be able to find creatures operating on the spiritual level. That makes sense, right?

The sensitivity of this spiritual awareness appears to vary from person to person. It should not be confused with the kind of extrasensory perception that has been routinely debunked by scientists. Your spiritual awareness of the presence of good or evil spirits will not help you to pick the ace of spades from a group of three face-down cards. That's material information, not spiritual.

On the other hand, this spiritual awareness might give you the strong impression that something very different is going on when you step inside a holy place like a Catholic Church versus an unholy place like a pagan temple. The environments might be very similar externally, but one is graced by the presence of Jesus in the Blessed Sacrament, and the other is filled with the demons that flock to idols. Our physical senses won't detect this difference, but our spiritual senses might.

If only that had been the last time that the devil attacked my son. While the night terrors stopped for the most part with that dramatic deliverance, he continued to have nasty temper tantrums. They were uncontrollable to the point that he expressed his desire to stop but couldn't. This time my antennae were up, and I could tell that something spiritual was going on, but I didn't know quite what to do.

Then I took my son on his first camping trip. He was four years old and super excited. We went fishing with five or six of my buddies and their kids. The night we got there, my son tripped and fell into a bed of coals prepared for cooking dessert with a Dutch oven. The coals gave him second-degree burns on both of his legs (blisters but no charring of the skin). After I finished tending his burns and gave him some painkillers to help him go to sleep, my brother-in-law remarked, "This kind only comes out with prayer and fasting."

You would think that this is a pretty weird thing to hear, but it struck me as right on. My son had never in his life been around an open fire and fell into one on his very first night camping. What if the temper tantrums were just a manifestation of a demon that was attacking my son by stirring up an emotional fire that he couldn't control?

I discussed it with my spiritual director a few days later, and I resolved that I was going to fast for my son to be delivered from the demon. I was going to give up beer and coffee for as long as it took. No deadline. At the time, I drank about a quart of coffee every day and the occasional beer. This fast would prove to be difficult. I told my son that I was going to give up two things I enjoyed to help him with his temper tantrums.

Within a few weeks, the change in his temperament was dramatic. The big out-of-control temper tantrums that had ruined everybody's day were gone. Not that he didn't have moments of sadness, or whining, or complaining. He was four. But the demon fled. I could tell. So could he.

"I want to give up milk," my oldest son informed my wife. When she asked why, he responded, "For my brother." He had felt such an improvement in his life during my fasting that he wanted to share the goodness with his younger brother making a sacrifice of his own. My wife and I were floored.

Now you might wonder why I didn't try to consult an exorcist during these experiences. Have you ever tried to FIND an exorcist? It's just about impossible. As far as I know, most exorcists (if a diocese even has an exorcist) keep their identity secret.

You might also wonder why I didn't take my son to a doctor. While I do believe that God heals miraculously, I do not reject good medical science. Remember what I said early on — I believe everything true. My son's behavior was not to the point that it was dangerous to himself or others, and so I thought that it fell into the realm of a parenting problem rather than a medical issue.

Besides, the tools of the psychiatrist can do nothing against a torment that is demonic in origin. Maybe they can offer some medication to numb the pain of a psychic disturbance, but a demonic affliction can only be eliminated through deliverance, fasting, and prayer.

So what my mother did for me, I did for my son. I prayed. I fasted. And I took him directly to Jesus for deliverance.

I also started to teach him about temptations and what to do about them. He listened. A couple of years after this, we were watching a movie together. I can't remember what.

He interrupted the film, "Dad, I think I'm being tempted."

I paused the movie. "Why do you think that?"

"I'm having all of these thoughts that say I hate Jesus and that it's all a lie."

"And it makes you feel really bad and sad inside?"

"Yeah. That's why I think it's a temptation."

"You want to pray against it?"

"Yeah." We prayed for a few minutes, telling the tempting spirit to flee in the name of Jesus.

"Do you feel better now? Is the temptation gone?"

"Yup." We turned the movie back on and finished watching it. I was so proud of him.

My goal as a father is to create an environment that will allow my children to flourish. Part of that is to help them discover and cultivate their natural talents, as well as strengthen and resist their natural weaknesses.

While I have to do continual spiritual warfare for them, I also have to teach my kids to recognize and avoid the snares of the evil one for themselves. I don't want them to be the weakest wildebeest in the herd forever. They have got to learn to fight lions for themselves.

My most important task is helping them to cultivate a personal relationship with God. It includes sharing what the Church teaches us about God and our faith. I need to help them embrace the rhythm of the Church's liturgical and sacramental life.

Even though they're still little, I try every day to teach them to be disciples of Jesus by showing them what it looks like to live a life of prayer and daily obedience to the promptings of the Holy Spirit. If I want them to learn to be holy, I have to strive for personal holiness. They'll do what they see their daddy doing, good or evil.

# CHAPTER 12

# Witness

*When he had risen, early on the first day of the week, he appeared first to*
*Mary Magdalene, out of whom he had driven seven demons. She went and*
*told his companions who were mourning and weeping. When they heard*
*that he was alive and had been seen by her, they did not believe.*

(MARK 16:9-11)

MARY MAGDALENE IS ONE of the most famous demoniacs
in history. Jesus cast seven demons out of her at some point,
though the Gospels don't describe what happened. I bet it
was pretty wild. Various commentators have speculated what
demons those might have been . . . demons representing the
seven deadly sins, all possible demons. We really don't know.

Her story teaches us a couple of important lessons. At the
beginning of this book, I said that casting out a demon is only
the beginning. It is far more important and difficult to KEEP
the devil out.

Mary's conversion didn't end with the exorcism. She couldn't
go on back to business as usual, doing the things that she did

before the demons left. Her life changed. She started to follow
Jesus. Sat at His Feet. Listened to Him. Ate with Him. Served
Him. She even followed Him to the tomb, seeking to serve
Him in death. God rewarded her devotion by making her the
first witness to His resurrection.

When the Lord came and spoke to me in the middle of the
night, I quickly realized that pretty much everything about my
life had to change. Vomiting out demons made this point very,
very clear. But change was hard.

I stopped listening to most of the music that I loved. Almost
all of my old friends stopped talking to me. No more late nights
at the bar or taking a new lady friend home for the night. The
flow of filthy words coming out of my mouth had to stop. All
that and more had to go.

But that wasn't enough.

I started a discipline of personal prayer. I returned to par-
ticipation in the sacramental life of the Church. I studied the
Bible, the teachings of the Church, and the writings of the
saints. I tried to cultivate virtues like purity, humility, patience,
gentleness. I became a beggar and servant of the poor.

Yes, casting out demons is dramatic and exciting — scary
sometimes. And growing in virtue is generally not exciting.

Nobody likes to get stuck in the middle of a montage. Sports
and action movies often contain a short montage or sequence
of images in quick succession that shows the training process.
I can think of a hundred examples. Chronologically, the montage might contain 95 percent to 98 percent of the actual time
covered by the story, while taking up only a minute or two of
screen time.

Growing in virtue, in holiness, is living out the montage.

It's 95 percent of the real work of being a Christian, and most of the time it's invisible to the naked eye. It's holding your tongue with a co-worker who makes you angry. It's getting up to put your toddler back to bed for the seventh time. It's turning off the television or walking out of the theater when the lead actress starts taking off her clothes. These moments are not dramatic, but these small victories add up during a lifetime. Satan is defeated in these invisible skirmishes. One day at a time.

Mary Magdalene was possessed by the devil before she encountered Jesus. Their meeting left her transformed forever. Not only was she freed from demonic influence and set on a new path of virtue, but Jesus later allowed her to witness His decisive victory over the Devil. She knew about the resurrection before everyone else, and she ran with great joy to tell the disciples that Jesus was alive.

And they didn't believe her. They went and checked for themselves. Well, at least Peter and John did. I don't know what the others were doing. Even when the two apostles looked into the empty tomb, they still didn't believe her. They didn't understand until Jesus showed up in person.

Why do I bring this up? I've just told you a bunch of crazy stories about how Jesus saved me from a bunch of demons and changed my life forever.

Now you've got to ask yourself the question, "Is this guy telling the truth? Or is he still crazy?" Maybe I only think I'm telling the truth. Maybe I'm like the guy in the retirement home who tells everybody that he's Elvis Presley or John F. Kennedy.

My favorite definition for sanity is the mental state where what you think matches what exists. If my stories are true, you might have to reevaluate a lot of what you think about the world. Am I a little bit crazy? Or are you?

I have good news for you. You don't have to believe me. It won't hurt my feelings. You can decide whether you think my story sounds true or not.

But don't stop there. If my story is true, it means that God exists, and He's interested in you. "Seek, and ye shall find." If you start looking for Jesus, for the God that I describe in this book, you will find Him. Or maybe more accurately, He'll find you.

If nothing else, do what I did. Ask God to prove to you that He exists. "God if you are real, if you exist, teach me." It's that simple. If He is infinitely powerful, then it should be easy for Him.

He stands at the door and knocks. Open the door. At least put your eye to the peephole.

See for yourself.

IF THIS BOOK BLESSED you or someone you love, please consider making a donation to Golden Harvest Food Bank at:

---

• www.goldenharvest.org •

---

Every dollar you give will provide $10 worth of food to families in need. Feeding the hungry changed my life. It might change yours, too.

*Just tell them Nathan sent you.*